STACK SILVER

GET GOLD

HOW TO BUY GOLD AND SILVER BULLION
WITHOUT GETTING RIPPED OFF!

HUNTER RILEY III

About The Author

Hunter Riley III spent many years on the trading floor in the rough and tumble pits of the Chicago Mercantile Exchange. He's been trading, investing in and buying gold and silver bullion for 15 years and is connected at the highest levels throughout the precious metals industry.

Hunter currently lives in his hometown of Chicago, IL for the summers and at an undisclosed location for the winters (Chicago only has two seasons).

For speaking engagements, book signings or if you have any questions contact Hunter through his Facebook page or website at:

www.StackSilverGetGold.com
or
www.facebook.com/silverinvesting

I Need Your Help......

Thank you very much for buying my gold and silver book! Could you please take a minute to REVIEW this book on Amazon because it will help me spread the word about buying gold and silver to people who aren't as smart as you? No big deal if you can't and thank you if you can! Believe it or not, your reviews really help me break through all the noise in the precious metals space.

www.stacksilvergetgold.com/review

Sometime in 2017 I will be releasing an online video training course on buying silver and gold bullion. As a thank you for buying my silver and gold book, I'm giving you full access to this online precious metals investing course at a huge discount. By the time you read this book it may or may not be available; either way, you can sign up for the early notification list or get the course at a huge discount if it's been released at this secret link (please don't pass this link out to your friends)

www.stacksilvergetgold.com/readerdiscount

Contents

INTRODUCTION

This is a short, no frills, straight to the point book that contains everything you need to know to start safely investing in gold and silver bullion today. Literally today, the day you read it. You'll find no pictures, no pretty artwork and not very little fluff. By reading this book, you're getting a crash course in gold and silver investing 101 that contains all my best knowledge I've learned through buying gold and silver for more than fifteen years. Unlike the other books in the precious metals niche, I'm showing you how to buy silver and gold bullion safely in the shortest amount of pages possible. If that scares you or if you'd rather read a book that rambles on for four hundred pages about the history of precious metals starting with how the Egyptians topped their pyramids with gold thousands of years ago, you can return this book; I won't be offended. The only history I deal with in this book is modern history. The history that directly affects you.

My name is Hunter Riley III; I spent seven years in the futures pits on the floor of the Chicago Mercantile Exchange with both brilliant and maniacal traders and have been investing in silver and gold bullion for the last fifteen years. You've probably realized, like I have, that buying gold and silver is a smart thing to do. If you would like more information on the exact reasons as to why you should invest in gold and silver, please see the "Do You Like Gold or Silver Better?" chapter question towards the end of this book.

My main aim of writing this book is to show you how you can safely and quickly buy gold and silver bullion without getting ripped off and becoming a victim of what's known where I'm from as "The Chicago Way." Whenever some dopey politician makes a promise to the citizens and ultimately screws them over in the end, we call it "The Chicago Way". Dead people voting. The Chicago Way. Friends of the Mayor getting lucrative city contracts. The Chicago Way. The Chicago Way usually involves the government, or a connected corporation and their cronies using the government, trying to slyly take something from you in one way or the other. Mainly your vote or your money. And maybe one day your gold and silver.

If you implement what you're about to learn in this book, you'll never have to worry about becoming a victim of "The Chicago Way" because ultimately you'll have gold and silver bullion as your back up and you'll know how to keep it out of their hands.

As gold and silver investing becomes more popular, more and more dealers and con artists are going to try to take advantage of you. There's so much nonsense out there, but gold and silver investing isn't really that difficult or complicated. This book is set up in simple question and answer format. At the end, you'll find your suggested resources directory. This directory will provide you with my best list of all the websites, books and services you'll ever need for your silver and gold investing.

Now before we begin, I'd like to tell you the powerful

analogy that originally opened my eyes to start investing in gold and silver. This is one of the very few times I discuss the "why" part of gold and silver investing in this book. I'm not telling this analogy to persuade you, I'm simply telling you this analogy so that you can use it to persuade people you care about to start investing in gold and silver.

Inflation is the devaluation of money through an increase in the money supply. Here's how it works. Imagine you have a mint condition Babe Ruth rookie baseball card and you are about to sell it at auction for $100,000. Before you sell it, some guy figures out a way to make exact copies of your Babe Ruth card and the copies are so good that there is no way you can distinguish between your original card and one of the copies. He then takes one million of the copies and throws them up in the air so that they all land on the auction table, right on top of your original Babe Ruth card. Now there is no way to tell which card was your original card. There are now millions of cards that are exactly the same!

Do you think you could still sell one of the cards for $100,000? No way in hell! Now that there are millions of these cards you will be lucky to get a fraction of what your card was originally worth. This is exactly what is going to happen to the dollar if the Federal Reserve keeps printing money! The dollar is just like the original Babe Ruth card in our example and I believe it will eventually lose its standing as the world's reserve currency and after that, eventually become worthless if they keep printing more and more dollars. In fact, the dollar is almost worthless historically. The dollar has lost 95% of its original value since the Federal Reserve was created in 1913!

If you save your money in dollars, you are slowly but surely losing them. One way to save yourself is to start converting some of your dollars into silver and gold bullion. Silver and gold are a hedge against inflation and unstable economies because they're considered real money. Moreover they are the only "currencies" governments can't print!

As of this writing, the United States is printing more money than the world has ever known. If you study history, you'll find that governments print money until it becomes worthless. Every single fiat or paper currency ever created in the history of the world has eventually gone to zero and become worthless. When that happens there is a huge transfer of wealth from the people with the paper money to the people with the real money, gold and silver. Which side do you want to be on?

After you have read this book, you will have all the information you'll need to buy real gold and silver safely today.

Now, let's get into it…

Hunter Riley III
Chicago, IL
February 2017

Chapter 1

WHAT ARE THE DIFFERENT TYPES OF GOLD AND SILVER TO INVEST IN?

When looking to make a gold or silver bullion investment, you'll find that gold and silver are available mostly in coins, rounds and bars.

Coins are most popular in the one ounce sizes but come in many different sizes and are made by an official government mint. They almost always have a date and face value amount listed on the coin. The United States coins are the best in my opinion. They are called United States Gold Eagles and United States Silver Eagles. Many other countries also mint their own gold and silver coins. Canada has the Maple Leaf, South Africa has the Krugerrand, China has the Panda, Austria has the Philharmonic and Australia calls one of their coins the Kangaroo. Most coins are made from at least .999 pure silver or gold. They're only .999 pure because many of these coins have a tiny bit of metal like copper in them to increase their durability. Because these coins are so beautiful and difficult to make and are legal tender, they have the highest premium; but this usually makes them easier to authenticate and more difficult to fake. I'll explain more about what premium and purity mean in a moment.

The main benefits of coins are that their purity and precious metals content is guaranteed by the government that makes them, they have a large secondary market, are simple to sell, don't require much authentication because they are so easily recognized around the world and some can be used as legal tender. The main drawbacks of coins are that, because of their higher premiums, you will usually be paying more money for your gold and silver than you would if you bought rounds or bars.

Rounds are coins that aren't made by a government. They are not legal tender and instead are made by private mints or refineries. They don't usually have a face value and aren't as ornate and well done as government minted coins, so the premium added on to rounds is smaller which means that you get more metal for your money. Rounds typically have the lowest premiums than any other form of precious metals except for the largest bars.

And bars, well, bars are bars. Bars can also be called ingots. They come in sizes ranging anywhere from about one gram to one thousand ounces or more! Since bars are sometimes so big, they are easier for the mint to produce and therefore have a lower premium added on than rounds or coins. But when you go to sell a big bar, dealers sometimes require them to be "assayed", or authenticated, which can add cost and time.

The main benefits of rounds or bars are that since they

have lower premiums, you're paying less over the spot price than you are for coins which means you get more precious metals for your money. The main drawbacks are that they are not as common as coins and may be harder to sell and need to be authenticated.

And finally we also have the junk silver. Junk silver is pre-1965 circulated US silver coins consisting of nickels (only 1942-1945), dimes, quarters and half dollars. Pre-1965 dimes, quarters, half dollars and dollars are made of mostly 90% silver. If you have any change lying around, check it out. You can collect it yourself or buy it in bulk. A one thousand dollar face value bag of junk silver contains about 715 ounces of silver.

What about the purity of gold or silver?

When considering gold purity, you want to pay attention to karats. A karat is the unit used to measure gold content or purity. The higher the karat number, the purer your gold. Since 24 karat is the highest karat number, 24 karat gold means your coin contains almost all pure gold with just a tiny amount of metal alloy. For this reason, 24 karat gold is any gold with a purity above .999 fine.

What does the "fine" mean?

Fineness is another way of relaying the purity of the gold. The fineness signifies the parts per thousand of pure metal in the alloy in proportion to its mass. There are many levels of "fineness." In addition to .999 fine or "three nines fine" there is .9999 fine or "four nines fine" and you can even sometimes find a coin that is .99999 fine or "five nines fine." Some examples of 24 karat gold coins include the Canadian Maple Leaf (.9999 fine) and the Chinese Gold Panda coin (.999 fine). 24 karat gold is the purest gold available, but it is softer and less dense than 22 karat gold which is used for some very popular coins. By the way, don't ever let anyone try to bait you into buying 26 karat gold. It doesn't exist. You may think I'm getting too deep in the weeds here but remember, the more you understand and know about gold and silver, the less likely people will be able to rip you off!

22 karat gold means your gold contains 91.67% gold and 8.33% other metals like zinc, copper or nickel. The coin is technically .9167 fine gold. Adding in these metals makes 22 karat gold harder, more durable and less likely to scratch. Some of the best known 22 karat gold coins are the American Gold Eagle and South African Krugerrand.

Even though a 24 karat gold coin will be more pure than a 22 karat gold coin, it won't always cost more. For instance, when you add in the premium you pay for a one ounce, 22 karat American Gold Eagle (.9167 fine), you're going to be paying more than you would for a one ounce, 24 karat Canadian Gold Maple Leaf (.9999 fine).

One more question you may have in your mind is does a 22 karat gold coin still contain an ounce of gold? The answer is yes! Both 24 karat and 22 karat gold coins contain one troy ounce of gold. The only difference is that the 22 karat coin weighs slightly more than a troy ounce due to the extra amount of metal alloy that is added to the coin in addition to the gold.

Silver also has some purity levels to pay attention to. Anything above .999 silver is known as fine (99.9% silver) or ultra fine (99.99% silver). These two numbers are what silver bullion traded on commodity exchanges and most silver bullion coins, rounds and bars are made of. For example, a silver Canadian Maple Leaf is designated "ultra fine" or "four nines fine" because it is made of .9999 or 99.99% silver, and a silver American Eagle is designated "fine" or "three nines fine" because it is made of .999 or 99.9% silver. You'll still be paying more for the American Eagle… so does it really make that much of a difference as to whether you should buy fine or ultra fine silver? Not to me. There is an argument to be made on a cultural basis. For instance, many Asian countries tend to have a strong preference for 24 karat gold instead of 22 karat gold. So, if you live in Asia, keep that in mind. In the United States or Europe, I have not noticed any major issues.

Keep moving down in purity and you'll find sterling silver or "925." Sterling silver is made of 92.5% silver and the other 7.5% contains various metal alloys like copper to increase durability. I think you're beginning to understand that the percentage of precious metal in a coin, like 92.5% sterling silver, can also be marked as 925 or .925 as this all means the same thing.

When you look at United States junk silver or silver in old coins, they usually contain about 90% silver (900) or below depending on their country of origin.

Finally, let's talk about a troy ounce.

Without getting into the history, the troy ounce is the

standard measure for precious metals like gold and silver and is not the same weight as a typical ounce, which is technically called an avoirdupois ounce. A troy ounce of silver does not weigh the same as an ounce of sugar. A troy ounce weighs 31.1 grams and a regular ounce of sugar weighs 28.35 grams. A regular pound of sugar weighs 16 ounces or 14.58 troy ounces. This might seem like a small difference until you get into larger amounts of weights and their prices. Sometimes scammers will try to sell you precious metals and charge you the troy ounce price for a regular ounce weight, so be careful! Always determine if dealers are pricing and selling in troy ounces or regular ounces. All you have to do to convert regular ounces to troy ounces is multiply the amount of regular ounces by .91.

Chapter 2

WHAT IS THE PREMIUM AND WHAT IS THE SPOT PRICE?

The spot price is the price at which silver or gold can be bought immediately, or the price at which silver and gold are currently trading at in the market. It is also the price that mints, and huge investors or industrial users pay for large quantities of silver or gold. So the prices you see quoted on financial websites and in the paper every day are based on the big 400-1000 thousand ounce bars or the prices of futures contracts. Smaller investors usually don't pay the spot price for silver and gold because mints pay extra money to turn the silver and gold into the smaller coins or bars that small investors want which adds a premium to the spot price.

The premium is the price that an investor pays over the spot price. The premium includes the cost of minting, marketing and distributing the metal and also the dealer mark up which includes their overhead and profit. Investors usually pay the smallest premiums on the largest bars because the larger the bar, the cheaper it is for the mint to make. The smaller the size of the silver or gold, the larger the premium because there are more expenses involved in making smaller sizes. It costs the mint more money to create a small coin than it does to create one 1000 ounce bar. This is similar to how a bulk store like Costco can sell you a box of 48 tubes of toothpaste for $48 while your local grocery store will sell you one tube of toothpaste for three dollars.

Premiums can vary by weight, mint, supplier, order volume, product and demand. Premiums fluctuate and usually are in the range of 1% to 40% of the cost of the gold or silver. Some dealers will have very high premiums and some will be very low. Also, the more scarce gold and silver become, the higher the premiums will usually be. At this moment, you really shouldn't be paying any more than a 1% to 9% premium, depending on the type and amount of gold and silver you buy and the market environment at the time of purchase. For instance, in the market crash and financial panic of 2007 and 2008, people were paying well above 10% premiums and waiting weeks for delivery if they could get their hands on any metal at all. Buy some now before the next panic arrives to avoid getting ripped off on premiums.

Usually, mints and refiners sell to wholesalers and charge them a premium, then the wholesalers sell to the retailers and charge them a premium then the retailers or dealers sell to you and charge you a mark up on top of what they paid for the metal.

Chapter 3

WHAT TYPE OF GOLD AND SILVER SHOULD I BUY?

If your aim is to invest purely in gold or silver, then you should buy strictly physical gold and silver bullion coins from national mints, or rounds and bars from the major refiners like Engelhard, PAMP, Johnson Matthey or Credit Suisse. You can also buy junk silver. When I say "physical," I mean gold and silver that you can actually touch. I'm not talking about paper gold like futures contracts or exchange traded funds (ETFs).

At first, stick to buying your metal from the national mints or the major refiners I mention. These minters and refiners are well-known and you are less likely to have a buyer who makes you go through the hassle of authenticating your metals when selling. Keep in mind the smaller the size, the easier it is to travel with and to quickly sell. Finding a buyer for your one ounce gold American Eagle worth $1200 is usually going to be an easier task than finding a buyer for your 32 ounce gold kilo bar worth $40,000. On the other hand, the larger the bar, the lower the premium you usually pay so you'll be getting more precious metals for your money. After you finish reading this book you'll have a pretty good idea of the pros and cons to owning smaller or larger sizes.

I personally have an assortment of large and small sized gold and silver bullion. I own junk silver as well as any silver .999 or above. As for gold, I own both 22 karat and 24 karat bullion.

I wish it was more complicated to explain, but it isn't. It's as simple as that. Here are some of my favorite forms of gold and silver bullion. And when I mention ounces, I'm referring to troy ounces.

SILVER COINS

American Silver Eagles

American Silver Eagles, sometimes known as American Eagle Silver Dollars, were created by the US Mint in 1986. They have an official one dollar face value and are considered legal tender. Every American Silver Eagle is made from one ounce of .999 fine silver and contains 99.9% silver and 0.1% copper to increase its durability. American Silver Eagles are shipped from the US Mint in boxes of 500 coins. In each box you'll find 25 tubes with each tube containing 20 American Silver Eagles. Each box weighs 42 pounds. Dealers will sell these Eagles by the box, the tube or even by the single coin.

Because of the beauty of these coins and the fact that they are legal tender, their premium is about 8% to 15% over the spot price of silver as of this writing. Occasionally, backdated or older Silver Eagles can be bought at lower prices than the current year's Silver Eagles. If you're buying Silver Eagles in bulk, make sure to ask about backdated Silver Eagles prior to buying the current year's Silver Eagles. American Silver Eagles also have a numismatic value to them; some of them can sell for way above their spot and premium price combined depending on the coin and its condition.

Also, because these are "legal tender" coins, they are exempt from IRS form 1099-B reporting requirements; dealers usually do not have to report the sale to the government when, or if, you sell them back unlike some other forms of silver. These coins are approved for individual retirement accounts (IRAs). Don't worry; we'll talk more about tax reporting and IRAs in the coming chapters. Silver Eagles have a high liquidity which makes them easy to sell. The US Mint frequently sells out of these "three nines fine" coins.

Canadian Silver Maple Leafs

This coin is the Canadian answer to the American Silver Eagle. Canadian Silver Maple Leafs are one ounce silver coins made by the Royal Canadian Mint and the government of Canada starting in 1988. They are legal tender in Canada and are one of the purest silver coins available containing a super high silver content of 99.99% silver (.9999 fine). Remember, people like us refer to this as "four nines fine" due to the .9999 fine silver content. They have a radial finish to them that makes the coins almost seem to glow. Maple Leaf's have some unique security features like micro-engraved laser markings and anti-counterfeiting technology where pictures of each coin are taken when they are minted and then encrypted and stored in a database. Dealers can quickly access this database to check the authenticity of any coin. Despite the fact that the Maple Leafs have better quality silver in them, their premiums are usually lower than American Silver Eagles. These coins have high liquidity, are IRS form 1099-B exempt and can be added to your precious metals IRA.

JUNK SILVER

Junk silver for the most part refers to any government coin which contains silver that has zero collectible or numismatic value over the value of the silver it contains. Circulated US coins minted before 1965 are the most popular form of junk silver today. These coins contain anywhere from 35% to 90% silver and include nickels from 1942-1945, dimes from 1892-1964, quarters from 1892-1964, half dollars from 1916-1969 (Kennedy half dollars from 1965-1969) and dollars from 1878-1935.

You buy junk silver for its "melt value" or what the coins would be worth if you melted them down and took the silver out of them. A $1000 bag (the face value of the coins in the bag) of US junk silver contains about 715 ounces of silver.

How do we know this?

At minting, these kinds of coins contained 0.7234 ounces of silver for each face value dollar. Over the years, it's agreed that the coins have lost some of their silver due to normal wear and tear. To make up for this loss of silver content, the gold and silver markets have set the standard that 0.715 ounces of silver is now the amount of silver contained in each face dollar of value which means that a $1000 face value bag of junk silver contains 715 ounces of silver. As of this writing, you can get a $1000 face value bag of US junk silver for about 1% over the spot price of silver. Make sure to keep an eye on the premium you pay per bag though because these coins are sometimes in short supply. When the supply dwindles, dealers charge higher premiums. The best US junk silver coins to buy are those made of 90% silver, the 1964 Kennedy half dollars, the 1946-1964 Roosevelt dimes and the 1932-1964 Washington quarters. Junk silver is not IRA eligible, but it is IRS form 1099-B exempt if you are selling less than 715 ounces.

SILVER BARS

I like silver bars because they have lower premiums than the government minted silver coins. The refiners who make the bars don't charge the wholesalers as much premium as the governments who mint coins do. This means you pay less money and get more silver than if you were buying coins. The bigger the bar, the more silver you get for your money. The price you pay for an ounce of silver in a 100 ounce bar is going to be a little cheaper than the price you pay for an ounce of silver in a 10 ounce bar. Many of the bars are IRA approved, very liquid and easily tradable, as well as IRS form 1099-B exempt as long as you sell less than one thousand ounces at a time. Unless suggested below, look to buy bars from major refiners like: Johnson Matthey, Pamp Suisse, Republic Metals Corporation, Sunshine, Engelhard, Asahi, Silvertowne and Royal Canadian Mint.

Royal Canadian Mint 850 Ounce Bars

If you've got a lot of money to invest and you want the cheapest silver, meaning silver that is marked up the least over the spot price, the Royal Canadian Mint (RCM) sells 850 ounce .9995 pure silver bars. These huge RCM silver bars have smaller markups than other forms of silver because you're buying in bulk. Each 850 ounce bar weighs about 58 pounds so make sure you have enough room to store them if you take delivery of your metal.

Speaking of taking delivery, since the RCM bars weigh only 58 pounds or so, you can ship them in US Post Office Flat Rate boxes, which is a relatively cheap way of shipping. If you instead bought 1000 ounce bars, many weigh over 70 pounds and are over the weight limit for the post offices flat rate shipping deal. The RCM bars have a low premium, are easier to move since they weigh much less than 1000 ounce bars and they happen to be .9995+ fine; most silver bars are .999 fine.

100 Ounce Silver Bars

I love the 100 ounce silver bars! They stack up very nicely, are easy to handle and store well in your safe. Each 100 ounce bar weighs in at 6.86 pounds and is made of at least .999 fine silver. These bars are easy to buy and sell. My favorite, and the coolest looking 100 ounce silver bars in my opinion, are from Johnson Matthey or Engelhard.

10 Ounce Silver Bars

10 ounce bars are also made of at least .999 fine silver. They're easy to buy and sell and are fantastic for stacking. I remember the first time I had enough 10 ounce bars to stack. Such a good feeling! You can get them from the major refiners and mints just as you would the 100 ounce bars. I personally like the Royal Canadian Mint 10 ounce bars. Silvertowne also makes some cool looking, hand-poured 10 ounce silver bars.

SILVER ROUNDS

Silver rounds are simply coins that are made by a private mint and not a sovereign state or government which means they are not legal tender. The main benefit of rounds is that you are paying a lower premium than coins. Some silver rounds are IRA approved and IRS 1099B exempt if you're selling less than 1000 ounces at a time. These include rounds from Republic Metals Corporation and Sunshine Mint.

Sunshine Buffalo Silver Round

The Buffalo silver round from Sunshine Mint is one of my favorite rounds. It is .999 fine silver and has the same Indian and buffalo images found on American buffalo nickels. Built into the round is a special "MintMark SI" anti-counterfeit technology that allows you to use a special decoder lens to verify the authenticity of the round. These silver rounds are IRA approved and IRS form 1099-B exempt if you're selling less than 1000 ounces at a time.

GOLD COINS

American Gold Eagles

American Gold Eagles were created by the United States Mint in 1986. Unlike the Silver Eagles, Gold Eagles come in four sizes and face values, a $50 face value for the one ounce coin, a $25 face value for the half ounce coin, a $15 face value for the quarter ounce coin and a $5 face value for the tenth ounce coin. The one ounce Gold Eagles are the easiest to find and they contain exactly one troy ounce of gold. American Gold Eagles are 22 karat gold (.916 fine) and contain about 91.6% gold and 8.4% copper-silver alloy. Remember that this added copper-silver alloy makes the coin more durable and causes all Gold Eagles to weigh a bit more than their stamped gold contents because they still contain one troy ounce of gold in addition to the added metals.

Like the Silver Eagles, Gold Eagles are legal tender but do not sell at their legal tender face value. American Gold Eagles are shipped from the US Mint in boxes of 500 coins. Each box contains 25 tubes, each containing 20 American Gold Eagles. Each box weighs 42 pounds. Dealers will sell these Eagles by the box, the tube or even the single coin. Due to their beauty and the fact that they are legal tender, their premium is about 8% to 15% over the spot price of gold, as of this writing. American Gold Eagles can also have a numismatic value to them. This means some of them can sell for way above their spot and premium price combined, depending on the coin, the condition and rarity. Also, like the Silver Eagles, because these are "legal tender" coins, dealers usually do not have to report the sale to the government when or if you sell them back unlike some other forms of gold. They are IRS form 1099-B exempt. American Gold Eagles are highly liquid, or easy to trade, and approved for individual retirement accounts as well.

American Gold Buffalo

In 2006, the US mint created the purest gold coin they have ever offered. Gold Buffalo's contain 24 karat, .9999 fine or 99.99% gold. Just to beat the lingo into your head a little more, because of this .9999 fine purity, we say the coin has "the four nines" or is "four nines fine." This is one of the purest gold coins in the world on the level with the gold Canadian Maple Leaf. On one side of the coin you'll see James Earle Fraser's famous design of an image of American Indian that is also found on old Buffalo Nickels. On the other side you'll see an American buffalo which was actually a real buffalo named Black Diamond who lived in the Central Park Zoo in New York City around the year 1900. These buffalo coins are IRA approved, IRS form 1099-B exempt and mostly come in one ounce sizes; although in 2008 the US mint did temporarily create a few other sizes.

Austrian Philharmonic

Although the US American Gold Eagle is the most popular gold coin in the world, the gold Austrian Philharmonic coin made by the Austrian Mint has the four nines (.9999 fine) and lower premiums. One side of the coin depicts the great pipe organ located in the Golden Vienna Concert Hall. On the other side you'll find various instruments used in Austria's famous Philharmonic Orchestra. These 24 karat sovereign coins are denominated in Euro's. You can add these coins to your precious metals IRA and they are IRS form 1099-B exempt. They are well recognized around the world.

GOLD BARS

Gold bars are on my radar because they have much lower premiums than government minted gold coins. There is a massive amount of wealth concentrated in a relatively small gold bar. Downsides with owning large gold bars include sometimes having to use the more expensive private shippers to move them (because the US post office only offers a maximum insurance of $50,000 per registered mail package) and a kilo gold bar currently has a value around $42,000 so you've got to ship them separately. You might also have to go through an extra assay or authentication process when you sell which could cost you time and/or money. Gold bars totaling one kilo (32.15 troy ounces) or more are IRS form 1099-B reportable when you decide to sell. Some bars are IRA approved and some aren't, so make sure to double check if you are planning to add to your precious metals IRA. Both sovereign and private mints make gold bars. A gold bar should have its purity, weight, refiner (maker) and a registration number stamped on its face. Only buy the gold bars with these markings as they are an indicator of legitimacy and quality. Below you'll find the sizes, brands and kinds of gold bars I like to stack.

Kilo Gold Bars

A kilo gold bar weighs a kilogram (32.15 ounces). It is made of 99.99% pure gold. The most popular kilo gold bars are made by the Royal Canadian Mint or the PAMP European precious metals refinery. The downside of kilo gold bars is that they may be harder to sell than the smaller gold bars because of their total price which, as of this writing, is around $42,000. For gold kilos, I prefer the Royal Canadian Mint bars. They are four nines fine and IRA eligible.

10 Ounce Gold Bars

10 ounce gold bars are easy to move and stack like pancakes. Many different minters make the ten ounce gold bars. These minters include PAMP, Johnson Matthey, Perth Mint and Engelhard. A 10 ounce gold bar is still quite expensive for the average person to buy so if you're looking to make an investment in gold less than a couple hundred ounces, it might be a good idea to buy the bars listed below instead. One of my favorite 10 ounce gold bars is the PAMP Suisse Lady Fortuna Veriscan. On the face of the bar you'll find Fortuna, the Roman Goddess of Fortune and Luck. The PAMP mint has this cool anti-counterfeiting "veriscan technology" built into the bar which will let you check its authenticity. The bar is stamped with a unique serial number, has the four nines and is IRA eligible.

100 Gram Gold Bars

100 gram gold bars are excellent for anyone looking to make a small investment in gold. Each 100 gram gold

bar contains 3.215 ounces of 99.99% fine gold and has relatively small premium. The premiums on these bars can sometimes be just a little more than the premiums on kilo bars which isn't bad. One of my favorites is the 100 gram gold "Combibar" from the Valcambi Mint in Switzerland. The gold bar is actually made up of 100, preformed, mini one gram bars that you can break off and use separately. So it's basically a 100 gram bar that you can easily break into one gram pieces. This bar is pretty convenient, has the four nines and is IRA eligible.

1 Ounce Gold Bars

You can find one ounce gold bars all over the place. The main reason you may opt to buy one ounce gold bars instead of one ounce gold coins like the American Gold Eagle or South African Krugerrand is that the premium for gold bars is lower. If I had to pick a favorite, I'd say the one ounce gold bars from the Perth Mint in Australia would do just fine. They have the four nines, they're IRA eligible and they even have neat little swans and kangaroos on their faces. As with all gold bars, as long as you're selling below a kilos worth of them, they do not trigger an IRS 1099-B form reporting requirement.

1 Gram Gold Bars

One gram is .0321 troy ounces of gold. I like buying some gold by the gram because you can get them cheap; currently the price of a gold gram is about $50, and if you're going somewhere where you'd like to keep a backup reserve of something other than cash, they travel nicely and pack a good store of value punch. The Perth Mint's gold gram is .9999 fine and IRA approved. When you get below an ounce in gold you do have to pay attention to the premiums though. Some premiums on gold bars or coins weighing less than an ounce can be absolutely ridiculous.

Chapter 4

GOLD AND SILVER SCAMS: WHAT KINDS OF GOLD AND SILVER INVESTMENTS SHOULD I AVOID?

First let me say that not all of the following are "scams." Some are just very easy ways for a beginning gold and silver investor to lose a lot of money. A more experienced investor could use some of these strategies to make an absolute killing. If you're a beginning precious metals investor, I think you should only concentrate on stacking up as much real gold and silver bullion as you can to start out. Once you have built up a nice little war chest of metal, then start learning how to use futures and options, or buy mining stocks. Don't make the same mistakes I did...get some physical gold and silver bullion in your hands first!

Silver and Gold ETFs (Exchange Traded Funds)

Silver and gold ETFs are basically mutual funds created to track the price of gold or silver except that they are traded the same as, and act very much like, stocks. ETFs are good for short-term trading, but do not replace buying real physical gold and silver bullion and may even be bad for long-term investing due to their high counter-party risk among other things. Counter-party risk is simply having to rely on someone else or another party (a supplier, bank or storage service etc.) to have your investment be good. If anything goes wrong with one of the parties you are relying on (your counter-party), your investment could become worthless or held back from you until the court system sorts the problem out. Some ETFs have up to seven levels of counter-party risk! Many people buy gold and silver as insurance against a huge failure in our financial system. To avoid getting ripped off when, or if, that happens, I suggest you stick to owning physical gold and silver with as little counter-party risk as possible. ETFs are a highly debatable topic and there are plusses and minuses for both sides.

When you invest in a silver or gold ETF, you're usually not fully investing in the physical metal. For instance, the iShares Silver ETF SEC filing states "iShares are intended to constitute a simple and cost effective means of making an investment similar to an investment in silver." This means when you usually invest in a silver or gold ETF, you are buying a share of a managed trust fund contracted with, or owned by, a bank that is set up to track the price of gold or silver. When you buy a share of the SPDR Gold Shares (GLD) ETF, you are purchasing a share that is approximately equal to one tenth of an ounce of gold. The GLD ETF has HSBC Bank listed as the custodian and the IAU ETF has JPMorgan Chase listed as the custodian. HSBC, in my opinion, is a bank that does not inspire honesty and trust. Just do a Google search for "HSBC money laundering" and you'll find multiple instances of this bank paying fines for money laundering for drug cartels, predatory lending practices and foreign exchange rate manipulation. Is this the kind of bank you want holding your gold?

Many experts believe that some of the banks don't necessarily own all of the physical gold or silver stated in the fund either and, if they do, the metal might not be insured. The only way to really know if they have all the gold or silver bullion they say they have is through daily audits of all counter-parties, custodians and sub-custodians during non-trading hours. On page ten of the 40 page GLD ETF prospectus, they begin to mention all the risk factors you must consider before making an investment in their ETF and, trust me, there are a lot of them. Here's one of my favorite examples of counter-party risk taken directly from the GLD ETF prospectus: "The ability of the Trustee and the Custodian to take legal action against sub-custodians may be limited, which increases the possibility that the Trust may suffer a loss if a sub-custodian does not use due care in the safekeeping of the Trust's gold bars."

Banks can also sell or lend out their gold and silver which could lead to "cross ownership" issues where multiple parties have been promised the same metal. Even worse, for a lot of these ETFs, if you aren't a dealer or own a huge number of shares (for instance a minimum of 100,000 shares of GLD), you can't redeem your shares for the physical metal. When you buy actual physical silver or gold bullion, you hold it outside "the system" either at your home stored in a safe or stored in a private vault depository and allocated in your name. We've all seen what has happened to some banks in the recent past and I frankly don't want any of them holding my gold or silver! There is just too much risk of a breakdown somewhere in the chain.

ETFs are good if the market runs as it should and liquidity abounds but, like Mike Tyson says, "Everybody has a plan until they get punched in the mouth." If anything ever goes wrong in the stock markets, if there is a panic, if silver or gold skyrockets or if the fund or bank collapses, or even a currency crisis happens, you might not be able to get a sell order in and you may not be compensated for your loss...after all, these are really just electronic entries on a computer. If our financial system shuts down for any reason, do you think you will be able to access your brokerage account? You don't have to worry about this if you have physical silver and gold in your possession or tucked away at a private vault depository carved into the side of a mountain.

Sometimes with ETFs you are also paying high annual ETF management fees as well as broker commissions and other sneaky fees which means the ETFs will return less over time than just holding the physical metal yourself. You may be denied access to your ETF because of bank holidays, acts of God, war, confiscation, stock market crashes, computer glitches, fraud, terrorism, hacking, cyber fraud, insolvency, lawsuits, liens, and more. If any of this happens with the ETF you invested in, you may be left with nothing more than worthless paper.

ETFs aren't very private either, and could be an easy confiscation for cash strapped governments. Another thing against ETFs is that you can only trade them for a limited amount of time, i.e., five days per week. This leaves you with some "overnight risk" as they say in the industry. Plus you have your usual reporting requirements regulated by the SEC and the Financial Industry Regulatory Authority which slows the roll on your privacy.

All that being said, I do dabble in ETFs from time to time and own some long term but I mainly use them for making short and medium term trades and some covered call options writing. You should only play with money you can afford to lose and only trade the ETFs that are the most liquid (the funds with the highest amount of shares traded per day) so you can get in and out of your position easily and quickly. And always remember, just because you own the shares of precious metals ETF doesn't mean you own the actual metal.

Some of the silver-related exchange traded funds include iShares Silver Trust (SLV), Global X Silver Miners ETF (SIL), PowerShares DB Silver ETF (DBS), Sprott Physical Silver Trust (PSLV) and the ProShares 2x Ultra Silver ETF (AGQ).

Some of the gold-related exchange traded funds include iShares Gold Trust (IAU), Sprott Junior Gold Miners ETF (SGDJ), Gold Miners ETF (GDX), SPDR Gold Shares (GLD) and the ProShares 2x Ultra Gold ETF (UGL).

Some ETFs such as the ETFS Physical Silver Shares (SIVR) or ETFS Physical Swiss Gold Shares (SGOL) are "bullion backed," meaning that they own the physical metals to back the fund entirely. I like these bullion backed ETFs for long-term plays. Some ETFs, like the ProShares 2x Ultra Silver ETF are "leveraged," which means that instead of trying to match the rise of gold or silver at a one to one ratio, they try to match the rise on a two to one ratio using futures or options; there is more risk and volatility involved. And some of these ETFs, like the Global X Silver Miners ETF, try to give you a return that corresponds to a specific group of mining stocks or metal producers.

Futures and Options

Listen up! Unless you're an expert or you're willing to put in the time and effort to learn and you have some money to burn, you'll want to avoid silver and gold futures and options too when you're beginning. I'm not going to get into exactly what futures and options contracts are, but essentially they are contracts that allow you to use leverage to achieve larger profits or losses. You pay less to control more. Futures and options can be good if you're actively trading gold or silver as they allow you to control a large amount of metal for a smaller amount of money than it would cost you to buy that amount of metal outright. On the CME Group's COMEX Commodities Exchange, a single gold futures contract lets you control 100 ounces of gold and a single silver futures contract lets you control 5000 ounces of silver.

However, futures are still part of the financial system and are regulated by the exchanges they are traded on. These exchanges can, and have, changed the rules of the game at any time they wish. For instance, the exchange could decide to allow sell orders only and say you can only accept a cash payout instead of the metal that the futures contract promises. Futures and options can also be subject to price freezes. This means that the exchange can cap the price of the futures contract and say it can only go so high even though the price of the actual physical gold or silver is going through the roof.

In addition, there are way more outstanding futures contracts than available physical gold or silver. If a huge crisis were to occur, and you were holding gold or silver futures contracts you would most likely be stuck with worthless pieces of paper. I hate to sound like a broken record but I always buy and hold physical gold and silver first. I temporarily trade the ETFs, futures and options. A popular saying in the gold and silver investing community is "if you can't hold it, you don't own it." Bottom line, with futures and options your losses can be magnified and the professionals will probably crush you anyway.

Un-backed Gold and Silver Storage

Morgan Stanley was caught and fined millions of dollars for charging their customers silver storage fees for silver that didn't exist. What does this mean? It means that if you call up certain firms and buy silver from them, they can take your money and not buy any silver. Instead, Morgan Stanley used that money for other non-silver related investments, the whole time charging their customers storage fees for silver that they weren't storing! More recently, in March of 2011, UBS was sued for selling silver they never owned and for charging "storage fees" for the silver they didn't own or have in their possession.

Now, eventually, if one of those customers called up and said they would like to have their silver delivered, the bank would have to go onto the open market that day and buy some silver bullion. This is a problem because if the price of silver takes off, they may not be able to buy any silver for you since all their customers will be asking for the same thing. The next thing you know, the company could go bankrupt like Lehman Brothers did and you will be left with nothing, or waiting in a long bankruptcy line with their other creditors!

Some banks will offer you unallocated gold or silver. How do you know? Many times you have to carefully read the contract. Unallocated, in this case, means that the metal is a liability of the bank. You don't really own the amount of gold or silver you bought but you are a creditor to the bank that may or may not be holding the amount of metal you bought. The bank legally owns the metal. There are no gold coins in storage with your name on them. All the gold and silver in the vault belongs to the bank and you own a piece of paper that says you are entitled to a certain amount. Sometimes, the problem with unallocated gold and silver is that it is very much like fractional reserve lending. A bank never keeps all the cash that their customers deposited in their vaults; they lend the majority of that cash out. Like our example with Morgan Stanley above, if everyone wants their gold and silver back at the same time, there's going to be a problem. As you'll later learn, unallocated gold and silver isn't always a bad thing, although in most cases I do not recommend it. It depends on your contract and the party you are doing business with.

Gold and Silver Mining Stocks

Gold and silver mining stocks are a double-edged sword. Some of them are amazing to own and a few of them actually outperform gold and silver at times! You can really feel like you've won the lottery if you pick a good one and it could be a hell of a ride. On the other side, some of them can be total scams run by complete fraudsters that end up going bankrupt.

The logical thinking behind investing in gold and silver mining stocks is that if the price of the metal rises then the price of the mining stock should also rise as well. This is sometimes true and it tends to be truer for the larger, more established mining companies.

For many of these miners though, the costs of operating the mine rise faster than the price of the metals. For example, the price of gold may rise which means the value of the miners gold deposits increases as well, but the cost of oil could also increase which would mean higher transportation and operating costs for the company. Workers can start demanding higher wages. Taxes can increase. Energy prices can increase. Soon, the rises in operating costs deplete any gains made by the rise of the metal price. To be successful with mining stocks, you really have to examine how the mining company management team is operating the business. Look for a management team with a successful track record and good fundamentals. The increase in the price of gold or silver should just be the icing on the cake.

Mining stocks are very susceptible to "pump and dump" scams and many times turn out to be nothing more than a hole in the ground with a liar at the top! The pump and dump uses beginning investors' lack of knowledge and experience against them. The scam goes like this: The fraudsters buy a ton of stock in a rarely traded or new mining company at a very cheap share price. They then pull out every trick in their sales and marketing arsenal to push this nothing company as the next big thing in the mining industry or the secret that you don't know about. They pay influential bloggers to write articles with headlines like "Best Gold Discovery Ever!" The new investors, who have not yet been around the block, see these marketing tactics and buy up the stock which drives up the price. The pump and dump originators can now cash out because there are now more people who want to buy their original shares at higher prices.

With gold and silver mining stocks, always perform due diligence and investigate the company you plan to buy shares in. Look at their management team. Do they have a successful track record or do they not really have a history, just some cool ads and online videos that seem to make sense? Remember that the blogs you read or precious metals newsletters you subscribe to can sell advertising space to advertisers that may not be fully vetted so make sure you do your own research carefully!

There are a lot of statistics we can use, but when you compare the Baron's Gold Mining Index (BGMI), which tracks the price of gold mining stocks, to the price of gold bullion over the last half century or so, you'll find that gold bullion has returned much more on average than gold mining stocks.

Gold and silver mining stocks allow you to leverage a rise in metals prices which could mean you'll make a killing really fast while even paying less for the privilege. Not so fast though! Unless you've got boat loads of cash you don't mind parting with, or you're willing to put in the effort and time to study the masters and become an expert yourself, the risk to reward ratio of investing in gold and silver mining stocks should mean it's a no go for you at first. Remember this example; silver bullion could soar but your silver mining stock could crater simultaneously due to a bad overall stock market or a bad management team running the mining company. If you do get into mining stocks, some of the best advice I've ever heard was to take some profits as soon as you get your first "double." This means once the stock you bought doubles, take out your initial investment and let the rest ride. You're now in the game with absolutely no risk.

Numismatics

Numismatics, or numismatic coins, are any coins that are collectible, historical or rare in some way. For just a pure silver or gold bullion investment, numismatic coins are not the way you want to roll. This is because there are three levels of cost included in each numismatic coin: The premium, the numismatic premium and the price of the silver, or gold, itself. When you buy straight gold or silver bullion coins, rounds or bars, you are only paying spot price plus the premium. Many of the premiums for numismatic coins are 30% to 60% higher than the cost of the actual gold or silver in the coin! The moment you buy a numismatic coin, you are already in the hole financially.

Numismatics, unless you luck out and find a really rare one, are also harder to sell back than straight bullion. You can sell your bullion back almost anywhere at spot price. If you want more for your numismatics, you've got to seek out an expert. Just try buying some type of numismatic coin off one of those Home Shopping Network programs and then try to sell it to your local coin dealer the next day. The results won't be pretty.

It is estimated that the vast majority of all counterfeit coins are numismatic coins and not bullion. The joke in the numismatics business is that all the money is made selling the numismatic coins to the beginner or non-collector. Sometimes the salespersons commission is even included in the price of the coin!

Watch out for the classic bait and switch scam in this area too. When surfing the internet you'll sometimes see an ad for gold and silver bullion at a very attractive price. When you click on the ad you'll be taken to a page that asks for your phone number or email address. After giving away your contact information, you'll eventually get a phone call from a very slick salesman trying to sell you the more expensive numismatics. Not all ads are like this but some are, so just be aware.

Every once in a while I'll listen to a salesman try to sell me numismatics and he'll pull out a chart that shows huge returns over regular gold bullion. The chart is probably cherry picked. They'll go back in history and find the one or two numismatic coins that had a great run and outperformed bullion. What they won't tell you is that the vast majority of numismatics don't compare to bullion. If you compare the professional coin grading service's 3000 rare coin index to the index of the spot price of gold since 2001, you'll find that rare coins have appreciated by about 36% and regular old gold bullion have gone up 345%!

If you've read all this and you still want to go into numismatics, the older and higher quality is better. Look for rare and high grade. You want to search for coins that are at least 50 years old. There's really no sense in buying a MS-70 2016 Gold American Eagle and then hope it becomes valuable in fifty years. Everyone is saving those coins now. You want to find the coins that weren't saved!

There are still plenty of people making a good living with collectible coins. Its wild west like atmosphere could get you some good deals. The guy to learn about rare coins from is Van Simmons, President of David Hall Rare Coins
www.stacksilvergetgold.com/davidhallrarecoins

But unless you are very interested in old and rare coins and history, and want to take the time to learn about what is valuable and what isn't, just stick to buying gold or silver bullion coins, rounds and bars. I find it fun to buy cool-looking pieces of gold and silver from time to time for my collection at home but I only buy the numismatics that are at bullion prices or very close to bullion prices due to the non-mint condition they are in.

Gold and Silver Pools, Certificates and Leveraged Accounts

Silver and gold pools or certificates are only just a

promise from the seller that they will deliver an agreed amount of gold or silver to the buyer at some time in the future. Like the un-backed silver and gold storage accounts, these guys can just take your money and use it for something other than buying silver or gold bullion.

When you ask for your metal, they could use new investor money to go out and buy silver or gold for you. When things are going well and good, this may work ok. But when gold or silver is on fire or there's a panic, more people will want to cash out than buy in and the entire pool or certificate program could collapse!

Like unallocated gold and silver, when you the buy into a certificate or pool program, the bank becomes the owner of your metal! So even if they did go out and buy the metal with your money, they still technically own it, not you. If the bank then gets into trouble financially, they can sell your metal to cover their losses. The bank would then probably pay you back in currency; not the metal you thought you invested in. But since the bank was forced to sell, you definitely wouldn't get the optimal price for your metal. Plus, there are a few more whammies against certificates and pools. The F.D.I.C. deposit insurance does not cover gold or silver. Your gold and silver in these accounts is co-mingled with other investor's metals.

I think you're getting the general idea now. When it comes to owning any type of precious metal, one of the major benefits is storing your investment outside of the financial system so that if anything ever gets too crazy, or Wall Streeters start acting like Wall Streeters, you have a safety net.

A leveraged account is where you put up $1000 of your own money and the broker loans you $4000 of their money to make your total investment in gold or silver $5000. It's leveraged because you're only using $1000 of your money to control $5000 worth of gold or silver. This looks like a good idea if you expect the price of gold and silver to go up. However, it may not be the smartest idea. Gold and silver are very volatile and if the price of the metal you bought goes down you could face a "margin call" in which you'd have to give your broker more money or have the broker sell your entire position to pay for the loss in their loan to you. They'd then give you the difference back - if there is any. Not only that but you have to pay ridiculous interest on the loan, as well as commission charges on the entire amount of your purchase. When all is said and done, you can lose way more than just your original investment with leveraged accounts. Leave the leveraged accounts to the professionals because that's who you're up against in this realm. They'll run you over.

Phone Dealers, TV Ads and Commemorative Coins

Remember this, many of these phone dealers just pitch nonsense that you don't need. They'll tell you some celebrity is endorsing their company. The celebrity is most likely paid for their endorsement and not an expert in gold and silver. Some dealers love to do the "bait and switch." You know of this by now. The TV ad will show very low bullion prices or some type of free offer or intro offer that will grab your attention. When you call up, they'll use sophisticated and psychological sales techniques to "upsell" you to the more expensive forms of gold and silver that are designed to make these jokers the most money, not you. Some of these pitches are so clever I'm even tempted to buy occasionally! But I don't. Now you won't either, will you?

When anyone calls you up to sell you "rare" silver or gold coins, hang up. People can blabber about anything on the phone. When they rip you off, it will be your word against theirs. The companies that run numerous TV, radio or magazine ads need to make a huge profit in order to pay for their advertising costs which ultimately means you are probably overpaying for your gold and silver.

Don't let these gold telemarketers scare you with words like "gold confiscation." Here's a brief history lesson on the topic of gold confiscation. In 1933, while the Great Depression was raging, President Roosevelt issued Executive Order 6102 and declared it illegal for Americans to own or "hoard" more than about five ounces worth of gold bullion or face a $10,000 fine and ten years in prison. Gold was never really forcefully confiscated though. First off, what a dumb deep state "government knows best" executive order. Save all the dollars you want because we can easily inflate the money supply and make your dollars worth less; but if you save gold and silver, you are an illegal hoarder. How dare anyone save gold and silver instead of dollars and actually make money while they inflate the currency.

During this time there were only a few prosecutions for violation of this order and the people weren't even convicted! Americans were allowed to sell their gold back to the government at the ridiculously low price of $20.67 per ounce. About nine months after gold was made illegal to own, President Roosevelt made the price of gold $35 per ounce. Anyone who had exchanged their gold for dollars just lost around 40% of their money. The good news was that many Americans just held on to their metal and didn't bother to sell it back.

This very un-American executive order was repealed in 1974. Here's the telemarketers secret trick. After getting you scared that the government could "confiscate" your gold coins again, they introduce you to special "non-confiscatible" gold coins that were exempt from being confiscated in the 1933 executive order. These supposedly non-confiscatible and non-reportable gold coins are usually pre-1933 US or European gold coins or modern day gold proof coins with ridiculously high premiums or price mark ups.

The only problem is that collectibles were never mentioned in the executive order and the term "rare and unusual coins" that was used was never actually defined. Don't fall for it; the coins they're trying to sell you are quite common old coins that they can make more of a profit on because they're considered collectibles and not bullion. Plus, government could always make you prove you are a legitimate collector and not just an investor. Stick to buying non-collectible, non-numismatic gold and silver coins, rounds or bars.

Could the government try to confiscate gold again? I think it's highly unlikely, but I never say never. What about silver? Actually, a year after the gold confiscation order was put into place; Executive Order 6814 ordered all silver be turned in for coinage creation. So, a silver confiscation could always be possible.

If you look at the gold confiscations that have occurred throughout the western world (England, Australia and the United States), you see that they occurred during times of economic crisis. I see some hard economic times in our future. Instead of confiscating gold, the government could institute some type of windfall profits tax on your precious metal gains. They did this in the 1980's when Congress passed the Crude Oil Windfall Profit Tax Act and taxed profits of oil producers. Whatever the case, I think chance favors the prepared mind so you need to plan accordingly. Gold jewelry was never confiscated so owning some of that may be a good idea. Setting up your own self-directed precious metals IRA is also a good way to avoid a possible windfall profits tax.

We'll talk more about that later on in the book but if you're just starting out, the most important thing to do first is start stacking some gold and silver bullion now and ignore potential confiscation. The government can't confiscate your imaginary gold. Eventually, you can use the tactics you learn in this book, as well as the websites I have recommended in the resources section, to store some of your gold and silver bullion in secure storage facilities overseas or out of reach of government hands.

A good question to ask anyone selling you gold or

silver is at what price he or she will buy it back from you if you wanted to sell it back to them the next day. If they say they won't buy it back or if they will buy it back for a lot less than what you bought it for, don't do business with them. When you buy gold and silver from a dealer, whether it is numismatics or bullion, there is a "bid" price and an "ask" price. The "bid" price is basically the highest price someone will pay for the metal and the "ask" price is the lowest price a seller is willing to sell their metal at. The dollar amount in between these two bid and ask numbers is called the "spread." Dealers make their money by buying the metal at the bid price and selling at the ask price; in other words, buying low and selling high.

As I write this now, the spot price bid on gold is $1238.40 and the spot price ask on gold is $1240.40 - the spread is only two dollars. If you were to buy gold at the spot bid price right now, you would only need gold to appreciate two dollars to break even. Not a bad bet.

But when you buy some of these numismatics or commemorative coins, or any metals over the phone (or even in person), some of the spreads can be so big that it may take you a long time to break even. Instead of just a couple dollars, some spreads can be hundreds of dollars apart. A lower spread usually indicates the coin is very liquid which means it's easier to sell to someone else when you finally want to sell. A bigger spread means the coin may be illiquid. So always keep the spread in mind when buying your metal.

Many companies which sell gold and silver on TV and over the radio have had class action lawsuits filed against them for deceptive business practices. When you get a chance, go to www.stacksilvergetgold.com/ baddealer to see an *ABC News Nightline* expose of a shady precious metals dealer.

Commemorative coins are usually only coated in silver or gold and are a sucker buy. Sellers try to get you all emotional by selling a commemorative coin that tugs at your heart strings while they sell you expensive paper weights. Beware of the "proof set" too. Most of these sets are uncirculated government coins in expensive packaging that are legal tender and contain no precious metal. In other words, a proof set featuring quarters from 1977 is just that - a bunch of quarters from 1977.

However, I do own a .999 silver one ounce coin that I bought more than two decades ago celebrating the first Cubs night game at Wrigley Field in Chicago. I think I paid $60 for the one ounce coin when silver was probably trading at five bucks an ounce! Eventually, I'll make my money back when silver goes through the roof but, for now, it's only worth about $18. The Cubs coin is pretty cool, and if they make another silver coin celebrating their 2016 World Series win I will definitely buy it, but if you're just buying silver or gold as an investment, you should stay away from commemorative coins.

Dealers may also try to sell you "mint condition" or "investment grade" gold or silver coins. An example of this would be a 2011 American Eagle gold coin rated MS-70 or Mint-State 70 which means the coin is in perfect condition. These mint condition bullion coins are usually marked up well above normal premiums.

The "MS" rating system is only important when you are dealing with very old and rare coins worth lots of money. Otherwise most coins that come straight from the mint are technically in mint condition; even if they aren't, it doesn't really matter to a bullion investor like you or me.

If you're going to buy collectable or commemorative coins, do research on the dealer before you buy. Check the dealer through the Better Business Bureau and do a Google search of the dealers name to see if they have a lot of complaints filed against them.

The Lowest Priced Dealers

I've seen many people get ripped off because they went with the lowest priced dealer above all else. The risk just isn't worth it in my opinion. The gold and silver industry is not federally regulated. The only state to regulate precious metals dealers is Minnesota so this means a lot of shady stuff can go on. Major dealers go bankrupt or steal from clients like you on a regular basis.

Northwest Territorial Mint: One of the most well-known and lowest cost bullion dealers filed for bankruptcy in 2016 and may have been running a Ponzi-like business. As much as 50 million dollars of orders may have never been delivered to customers. This Washington, Texas and Nevada based dealer had an F-rating by the Better Business Bureau with over 70 complaints filed. You can read more about the ordeal here:
www.stacksilvergetgold.com/northwest

Bullion Direct: This huge, low cost online dealer filed for bankruptcy in Austin, Texas in 2015. Over 6,000 people lost a lot of money in this debacle. Customers bought and stored metals with this dealer and then out of the blue found out that the metals they thought they had stored never actually existed. When a customer bought metal and asked for it to be stored, Bullion Direct just took their money and never bought any metal. Read more about it here: www.stacksilvergetgold.com/bulliondirect

The Tulving Company: These very popular scam artists went bankrupt in 2014. They were one of biggest and the lowest cost dealers you could find on the internet. Some of their almost 30,000 customers noticed the delivery times for the metals they bought getting longer and longer. Normally, delivery shouldn't take more than a week. Tulving was passing three to eight weeks delivery time in a normal market environment. Their complaints started to rack up with the Better Business Bureau to the tune of almost 200 until finally they shut their operation down. Many experts just think the company outright stole almost 50 million dollars from customers. The owner ended up pleading guilty to wire fraud and the people still haven't gotten their money or metals back. Read about Tulving here: www.stacksilvergetgold.com/tulving

KITCO: I get asked daily about KITCO because they are a very popular Canadian precious metals dealer due to their marketing and reporting. KITCO has some free resources like precious metals charts and spot prices that I occasionally use. But do I buy gold and silver from them? Nope. Why? Because they have been under Canadian bankruptcy protection for years and are under fraud investigation from the Canadian version of the Internal Revenue Service. KITCO is contesting the charges but as it stands there is no way in hell that I am going to risk letting them handle my metals or money. Read more about it here: www.stacksilvergetgold.com/kitco

If you don't want to get ripped off, you need to look for honest and reputable traits in the company you buy your precious metals from other than just who has the lowest price. Honesty, reviews, complaints, reputation, years in business, delivery times and more must to be taken into consideration to avoid getting ripped off!

Chapter 5

HOW CAN I AVOID BUYING FAKE GOLD AND SILVER?

The bad guys are getting smarter. Today, there are factories in China pumping out fake gold and silver bars and coins.

The biggest source of fake bullion seems to be coming from Chinese wholesalers. They now make fake versions of almost all national mint coins, as well as the collectible numismatic coins.

The fake bullion is usually plated in real gold or silver and then filled with some kind of base metal, like copper. What you'll also find these tricky bastards doing is creating a bar with a thick layer of silver or gold but then hollowing out the inside and filling it with tungsten rods. Tungsten has a density that is very similar to gold. This method can even fool some x-ray machines!

So how do you know if you're getting the real thing?

Buy from a trusted dealer who only buys directly from the mint or refiners. Research your dealer, make sure they don't have a million consumer complaints against them and ask what strategies they use to make sure they don't sell you counterfeit gold and silver. Double check that any secondary metals (metals bought back from customers or other sources besides directly from the mint or refiner) are properly assayed and/or x-rayed.

There are various gold testing kits and devices you can buy online, although I have not personally used any. Some local jewelers can test the purity of your gold and silver. Just give them a call and ask. One method you can use to test out your gold or silver to see if it's real is the ping test. When you tap two coins together you'll hear a "ping-like" sound. Counterfeit gold or silver coins will give off a higher pitched and longer lasting ping than the real gold and silver. Go to Google and search "how to ping test gold and silver" and you'll find many video examples. It's not an absolute test, but it will give you an idea.

You also want to compare the edges, the markings, the dimensions and the "relief" of the metal to another of the same piece of metal that you know to be real. Do they look the same? For instance, the relief of the coin refers to the height of the image on the coin. The relief on a fake coin is usually too high or almost flat.

Again, don't let any of this stop you from stacking gold and silver. All you have to do is buy precious metal from a reputable dealer instead of eBay, and avoid anyone trying to sell you gold or silver below the spot price. For updates on all the latest tricks that the scammers are using visit www.stacksilvergetgold.com/spotfakegoldsilver

Chapter 6

SHOULD I BUY FROM A LOCAL OR AN ONLINE DEALER?

I buy from both! Keep in mind, just because one dealer has a lower price than another doesn't necessarily mean that is who I will buy from. Low prices sometimes mask the fact that the dealer has a bad reputation. As you've learned, dealers can also offer low prices then fail to deliver or go bankrupt. In most cases I will buy from a dealer with an honest and established reputation, even if it means paying a little more. Let's go over some of the differences between local and online dealers.

Local Dealers

The best thing about a local dealer is speed and anonymity. You can head over to their shop and buy some metal immediately without anyone knowing about it. You can also get to know and trust exactly who sold you the metal. You don't have to incur other expenses for shipping and insurance to get your metal and you can sell it back to your local dealer just as quickly as you bought it. Another thing I like about my local dealer is that he always has unique pieces of gold and silver. This might not make sense to you now, but after collecting for a decade you are going to want to find some variety. Another thing I love about local dealers is that as long as you don't purchase too much gold and silver at any one time with cash, your purchase is totally private and anonymous. There is no way for anyone to really track what you're doing, so you can stack in secret. As rules may change, just ask the dealer how much metal you can buy without reporting and buy below that amount at any one time.

However, buying from your local dealer means premiums are applied when you buy and sell your metal. Usually you pay a larger premium at a local dealer and get back a smaller premium when you sell than you would with an online dealer. Local dealers may not have the specific amount or type of gold or silver you want to buy. I've made big buys from local dealers before that consisted of 30 or so different forms of the same metal. Local dealers buy a lot of their metal second-hand, from private customers like you, so there is a little more risk than if you were buying metal from an online dealer who gets it directly from the mint.

How do you find a good local dealer?

You can check with the US Mint here www. stacksilvergetgold.com/dealerlocator to find dealers near you. If you're in Europe or Asia many banks sell gold and silver! Another way to find a local dealer is good old Google. Go to Google and type in the search box "coin dealer Chicago", or whatever city you happen to live in. If there are many dealers within driving distance, go and check all of them out. Look at their online reviews. Maybe make a small purchase from each shop and see how the service is. Talk to the dealer and ask questions. See if the dealer is willing to give you a good piece of advice (that you've learned in this book). Does the dealer seem honest or are they trying to "up-sell" you into a higher priced item that you don't need?

Online Dealers

What I like most about online dealers is that many of them, at least the most reputable dealers, get their metal directly from where it is produced. Sometimes it's even shipped to you directly from the mint or refinery. You also tend to pay less for your gold and silver even after you include shipping and insurance, provided you order enough metal. You can put in an order at any time of day and buying the same kind of metal in bulk is easy. Make sure your dealer is transparent and posts their prices and all associated fees like shipping and insurance costs and credit card or bank wire charges on their website. Confirm how long delivery is expected to take as well.

Just like with local dealers, you want to shop around and look for a dealer who also tries to educate you rather than a dealer who is pushing you to buy the most expensive metal. When you buy a lot from an online dealer you'll probably have to use a cashier's check or bank wire to avoid huge credit card fees. You'll have to wait until your check clears for your metal to be shipped.

Chapter 7

HOW AND WHERE SHOULD I STORE MY GOLD AND SILVER?

I'm going to start this chapter off by ordering you to store your gold and silver in multiple locations! Start storing your metal in your home first. But, as you stack more silver and gold, you have to think about using private, non-bank storage facilities and "internationalizing" your gold and silver bullion. You want to spread your storage risk out so that if one location becomes unavailable you have others to go to. Let's get into it.

When you're first starting out, the best option is to store your gold and silver bullion in a location where you have the most control over it and keep it out of places where others, like banks and governments, can control it. When governments get in trouble financially, they start doing some nutty things. They implement cash or capitol controls that restrict, control and tax the flow of money into and out of their country. Just take a look at what happened to the citizens of Cyprus in 2013 or the 2016 war on cash going on in India and other countries. There is a growing war on cash in which governments are trying to get rid of, or reduce, the size of paper currency. Governments across the world say they are doing this in the name of fighting corruption, drug dealers and terrorists. Don't buy it. Government debt across the globe is astronomical. Governments ultimately want your money to be in digital form because it is easier for them to control and tax without your permission. When governments implement capital controls, it's the savers who get hurt the most.

When you buy your gold and silver bullion for the first time, you either want to "take delivery" of some of the gold and silver if you purchased it from an online dealer or walk down to your local dealer and buy some to take back home with you. I remember that magical feeling the first time I held some of the silver I bought in my hand. At that moment, it was like everything came together and I fully understood why it was so important that I was stacking up some gold and silver. I was trading some paper (in the form of US dollars), which throughout history has always eventually become worthless to whichever country issued it, for something that has stood the test of time as a store of wealth and purchasing power for thousands of years. Once you build up a good war chest of metals stored in your home, it's time to optimize your storage and add private non-bank allocated custodial storage and offshore safe deposit boxes to your arsenal of storage locations.

I first want to stress that, as a gold and silver stacker, you must stay under the radar! Never brag to your friends about your stack. Don't show people your cool home safe set up. And for the love of God, or whomever you pray to, don't post pictures of large amounts of precious metals on Facebook or other social media accounts or internet pages. Stay under the radar and make sure you keep out of the public limelight.

Home Storage

You can store your gold and silver bullion at your home in many different ways, but whichever way you choose to store it, keep it hidden and not out in the open. I'll get into a bit more about home safes in the next chapter but it's a smart move to keep your home safe hidden as well. You want as many layers as possible between your home safe and the visible world. In other words, don't just get a safe, put it in your master bedroom and leave it at that. Robbers love master bedrooms. Get a safe, put it in a hole in your floor, cover that hole up with a door in the floor, put a rug over the door in the floor and then put a giant piece of furniture on top of the rug. In short, you want multiple layers of invisibility.

You need to think out of the box when it comes to storing your metals at home. So where are some places to hide your metals at home?

Before you start hiding your metals, you want to shield your metals by putting them in a protective plastic tube or casing to keep them untarnished and in good condition. Depending on where you hide them, you may also need something waterproof as well.

Some of my favorite places to hide my metals in my house, besides my hidden floor safe, are fake or hollowed out books. I have a big library and a few of the books in the library are fake and actually contain gold and silver bullion. You'd never even think twice if you looked right at them. Book safes are fantastic. I also store some gold and silver in my freezer! I emptied out a large container of a horrendous flavor of ice cream and replaced the insides with many waterproof, plastic tubes of gold and silver coins. My friends have gone even further and have frozen some of their metals in blocks of ice stored in a second freezer.

Other ideas for storing and hiding your gold and silver include hollowed out "pet" rocks, the bottom of cat litter boxes, paint cans, a waterproof container or PVC pipe buried a few feet down in the ground, fake hollowed out logs in your woodpile, at the bottom of flower pots, false piping and even in a compartment under your fireplace. It may also be smart to have a slightly visible "decoy stash" in your home made up of a few pieces of silver if you think that many people know you keep lots of precious metal at your house.

One question I get asked a lot is should you insure the gold and silver you store at your home? I personally do not. When you get a home policy to insure your precious metals, there are just too many people who will know that you store gold and silver at your home. Your insurance agent and others in their office will know. The appraiser and others in their office will know. You're not staying under the radar if you insure your metals at home.

Safe Deposit Boxes

When we start talking about safe deposit boxes, there are two kinds to consider. A safe deposit box at a bank and a safe deposit box at a private storage or vault company.

Bank safe deposit boxes are my least favorite. Banks in the United States are part of the financial system. If something major happens, you might not be able to get your metal out when you want. Banks are subject to the will of the government and generally want as much control over your wealth as possible. This means you can face bank holiday and seizure risk, as well as banks cooperating with government information requests without your knowledge… which they do on a daily basis in the United States.

More recently, we've seen documented instances of banks losing customers safe deposit boxes and some banks are now instituting policies of disallowing cash or coins to be stored in the boxes. Even though getting a safe deposit box is as easy as walking in to your local bank, I'd stay away from using bank safe deposit boxes because there are just too many issues that could arise and prevent you from getting access to your metals.

If you are going to use a safe deposit box at a bank, get the contents of your box appraised by someone like a jeweler. Make sure you confirm with your insurance company to find out whether they would insure the contents of your box because your bank safe deposit box is not covered by FDIC insurance and you want to be protected in case they get robbed or lose your box. Check in on the box a few times per year to make sure it hasn't disappeared and think about telling a trusted family member about the box just in case something happens to you. Remember what happened to Robert DeNiro's character in the movie Casino! However, don't go too crazy and give someone else the only key!

My unfavorable view of bank safe deposit boxes doesn't mean all safe deposit boxes are bad. Let's take a look at private safe deposit boxes.

Private safe deposit boxes are the way I roll. For the record, when I say "private" I also mean non-bank. Private, non-bank safe deposit boxes are probably the most under-the-radar option for storing your gold and silver besides burying it somewhere in the woods and using a treasure map to find it. All you have to do is rent a safe deposit box from a private storage or vault company. Going offshore to do this is even better and more private (more on this in a minute). Private safe deposit boxes aren't controlled by any bank and if the markets crash, you don't have to be afraid that you won't have access to your box due to a bank holiday or government asset seizures.

Even better than your typical private safe deposit box are private foreign safe deposit boxes! Going offshore to set up a private safe deposit box to store your metals can be done entirely under the radar. They are not easily reachable from prying hands, seizures or frivolous lawsuits. If all hell breaks loose in the United States, you'll have a good amount of valuable metal stashed away in another country to fall back on. Just make sure you set up your private foreign safe deposit box in a country that you wouldn't mind visiting for a while.

How do you even get a private foreign safe deposit box (PFSDB)?

It's pretty easy. First, you have to ship some of your metals overseas (which is actually becoming harder and harder as time goes by) or you have to travel to the country where you're setting up your box and buy some gold and silver locally. If you choose to ship your metal, refer to the recommend shippers in the resources section of this book. If you're going to attempt to actually transport some of the gold and silver yourself, check all the customs regulations in each country you will be passing through in your travels or, even better, get a nonstop flight.

Probably the best way to remain anonymous and fill a private foreign safe deposit box up with gold and silver is to first set up a PFSDB and a bank account in the country you choose to store your metals. Then, wire cash to that account. Fly over to that country and head straight to the bank. Withdraw your cash and go buy some gold and silver. If you're in a country like Austria, you can buy it directly from the bank. Once you've purchased your metals, head over to your PFSDB and load it up.

There are a few traits to look out for when selecting your PFSDB. Ideally you'd like to use a company who has been in business for a long time and has an established and honest reputation. They must also have highly secured storage facilities. The location of your PFSDB, with few exceptions, should be in a country with a history of stable government and relative financial secrecy and respect. I recommend setting up your PFSDB in countries that have a solid history of honest metals storage like Singapore, the Cayman Islands, Switzerland, Austria, Australia and more. You'll find all my recommended countries in the resources section.

Private Custodial Vault Storage

Private custodial vault storage is how I store my metals after I've built up a war chest in my home. Once you buy gold or silver from an online dealer, some of them will only ship it directly to you. Some of them will also store and secure it for you. As a custodian of your metal, they can also sell it on your behalf. These companies can be US or foreign based. I use both; check the resources section again for my recommendations.

Something to be aware of concerning these kinds of companies is if, in addition to storing your gold and silver, they also lease or sell gold and silver. This could be a problem because some companies may decide to sell or lease some of the metals they are storing for some quick cash because they believe that every one of their customers will not ask to take their metals out of storage at the same time. If a big market move occurs, the company might not be able to buy back the metal they sold and then you could be out of luck. Do some research and make sure your storage company has policies that prohibit this. Make sure the company you choose stores your metal in a fully insured and secured vault. Ask to see proof of insurance too. Let's go over some different kinds of private custodial storage now.

Allocated and segregated vault storage means that your metals are stored separately and titled under your name at a secured vault, usually operated by an expert security company like Brinks which your custodian has contracted with. The exact pieces of gold or silver you buy from the dealer are put into a secure container, sealed and stamped with your name and account number. For a small monthly fee (usually), your custodian secures, separates and stores your metal for you. You can have your metals delivered to your home at any time or, as your custodian, they can sell your metal on your behalf at your direction and transfer the cash directly into your bank account or mail you a check. Another cool thing about these private custodial storage options is that when the terrorist attacks of September 11th happened, all the banks shut down and ATM's ran out of money. But guess who was open? Private storage companies like Brinks.

Allocated, un-segregated vault storage is almost the same as allocated/segregated except that you have ownership title to the amount in ounces of gold or silver you deposited or purchased but not the exact pieces. This is much better than a pooled, unallocated or comingled account because you are listed as the rightful owner. Your metal is not listed on the company's balance sheet and it is titled in your name. The vault stores tons of gold and silver and you own a certain amount of it but they don't specifically put your metal in its own little box with your name on it. Because of this, the storage fees are usually cheaper than with segregated storage.

Some custodians may charge a "fabrication fee" for turning your metal into smaller forms when you decide to take delivery of your metal from an un-segregated account. Another drawback of un-segregated storage options is that there is a possibility you may face a delivery delay if everyone is trying to get their metal at the same time in the event of a crisis.

With both segregated and un-segregated options, make sure the procedure to sell your metals or take delivery of your metals is a quick and easy process without many hoops to jump through. Have some of your metals delivered to your home if possible to test out their delivery process. Maybe sell an ounce of silver as well.

So, what is the difference between allocated and unallocated gold and silver?

"Allocated" means that your gold and silver is not listed as an asset on the custodian's or storage company's books. It's not a liability of the bank or vault company. The gold and silver is legally yours and titled in your name. If a bankruptcy were to occur with the company, the government or creditors can't touch your metals. Always use allocated for long term storage.

In most cases, "unallocated" means that your gold and silver is a liability of the business that offers it. You don't legally own the metal! Unknown to most people, this is probably the way most gold and silver is "owned" by the public. If a bank has your unallocated gold, they can lend it out to someone else! If the business holding your unallocated gold goes bankrupt, you have to get in line with all their other creditors and may only get a tiny bit of your investment back. If there is a financial crisis, your unallocated gold may very well be in trouble. Never store any unallocated gold or silver unless you are just planning on trading in and out of a position and selling it back very quickly. If you run into a dealer you love who doesn't offer allocated storage of some kind, just have the metal delivered to your house instead. If you insist on an unallocated gold and silver program, check out the program at The Perth Mint. But you should just listen to me and use unallocated for short term storage and trading only or better yet, not at all.

Your initial storage goal should be to store a good amount at your home. Then start storing your metal with a US-based custodian who contracts with a private vault. Finally, try to move some of your metals to a private foreign safety deposit box or vault to truly "internationalize" your gold and silver holdings and protect yourself. You'll find my recommendations in the resources section.

Chapter 8

WHAT TYPE OF SAFE DO YOU STORE YOUR GOLD AND SILVER IN?

I got my safe from Safes Direct which you should be able to find at www.stacksilvergetgold.com/safesdirect and my particular safe is called a "Jewel Vault TL-30". Jewel Vault also makes other safes such as the TL-15 or the TL30X6. These safes are thick and strong with huge locking bolts. They also have a feature that includes inner dual plates of tempered glass that activate two randomly located relocking devices in the event of a burglary attempt. I paid about $1800 for my safe. You don't need to go this crazy with your safes though; any safe will do as long as it's secure and well-hidden.

Depending on the amount of gold and silver you store at home, a good safe can cost anywhere from $500 to $100,000 or more. You can find a good "used" safe on Craigslist or eBay. I said earlier, it is a good idea to keep your safe out of sight. Put it in the floor and put a piece of furniture over it. Google "floor safes" or "hidden safe" and you'll find many different ways to hide your safe.

At the very least, get one of my favorite "book safes" for your first 300 ounces of metal. This will do just fine;

surely some of the last things a burglar looks at are your reading materials!

Chapter 9

CAN I ADD PHYSICAL GOLD AND SILVER BULLION TO MY 401K OR IRA?

If you want to own gold and silver without getting ripped off, fantastic news came in 1997 when gold and silver bullion were approved for IRAs. Not every IRA custodian allows this though, so if yours doesn't, you may want to switch to one that does. Creating a self directed IRA could help protect you from possible windfall profit taxes or even the government nationalization of IRAs. This will make your IRA one step removed from normal and first to be targeted "herd" IRAs and harder to tax. You may be able to roll over all, or any portion of, your current IRA into a precious metals self-directed IRA.

What is a self-directed IRA? A self-directed IRA has the same basic rules as a regular IRA but you can add investments like real estate, gold and businesses in addition to the stocks, bonds and mutual you invest in with a traditional IRA.

I like these because you get to buy gold and silver using the tax benefits of an IRA! The fees for most people's gold and silver IRA should be around a couple hundred dollars per year, with storage costs included.

If you have a 401k, you will only be allowed to purchase "paper" gold or silver in the form of ETFs or mutual funds. Remember from previous chapters on why owning strictly paper gold could be trouble?

Find out if your 401k is eligible for an "in service roll over." An "in service roll over" could let you transfer some of the money going to your current 401k to a new self-directed IRA. Also, if you ever leave your current place of employment, you'll have the option of rolling your accumulated savings into an IRA.

You can add physical American Gold Eagles or any other gold coins that are at least .995 fine to your IRA. You can also add some gold bars since most gold bars are 99.99% fine. Old US gold coins and Krugerrands can't be added to your IRA because they are less than .995 fine gold.

For silver, you can add American Silver Eagles, other government minted silver coins or even silver bars to your IRA. Like the gold, the silver coins carry higher premiums. So if you're going to be adding in bulk to your IRA, buying silver in ten, one hundred or even one thousand ounce bar form is usually the way I like to go. Junk silver is not currently allowed in an IRA. If your IRA doesn't allow gold and silver purchases, the websites I have mentioned in the resources section will help and direct you to some quality IRAs that allow gold and silver purchases. Just pick a silver and gold IRA custodian to set up your IRA, then transfer the money into your account to buy your metals and then select a third party private vault depository for storage.

One caveat: IRA specialists usually suggest buying

metals with your IRA when you already have IRA funds you can roll over. Otherwise, if you start a new IRA with a yearly contribution of a few thousand dollars or so, the annual storage fees for your precious metals would immediately begin to eat into your retirement savings.

Some of the benefits of a precious metals individual retirement account include avoiding capital gains taxes when you go to sell your gold and silver, taking possession or transferring your metals tax free and protecting your gold and silver from creditors if you go bankrupt or face a lawsuit. Each state has different guidelines, so make sure to check with your specific state. And if you do decide to have the metals in your account shipped to you, you will need to fill out a withdrawal form and you'll get a 1099-form for the value of the metals at the end of the year.

A downside of a precious metals IRA is if you're under 59 and ½ years old, there's a penalty for cashing out.

Another aspect of a precious metal IRA that I like is the privacy. At the end of each year, your IRA custodian must disclose your name, address, social security number and total value of your account but not necessarily what you have in your account which could be gold, silver, businesses etc. No one needs to know you own metals. Another good thing is that your custodian will value your account based on the spot price of the metal. So, if you also fill it with some coins like American Eagles that have higher premiums attached to them, your IRA will hold more value than stated.

One quick word on annuities since I see an obvious

way an annuity owner can get "ripped off." If you or someone you know has an annuity, the most important thing you must protect your annuity from is inflation because they always lose out with inflation. Your payouts are worth less in an inflationary environment. Own some gold and silver to protect and hedge your annuity from bad inflation.

Chapter 10

CAN I TRAVEL WITH GOLD AND SILVER?

Yes you can...but does that mean you should? The answer is a big no in most circumstances.

State to state travel by car, train or plane is pretty simple, with the most important thing to keep in mind being security. You may also want to be aware of civil forfeiture laws where essentially law enforcement officers can seize your assets if they suspect you of some type of wrong doing. They don't even have to arrest you or charge you with a crime to take your stuff. A quick Google search will show some recent and horrific examples of this nonsense happening to innocent people. That being said, I still load up my car with some precious metals to take across state lines to another property I own on a fairly regular basis.

If you're traveling in and out of the United States, you must declare if you are carrying $10,000 or more on your way out or in to the country. Now it used to be that, technically speaking under legal tender law, a one ounce American Gold Eagle coin only has a face value of $50 and a one ounce American Silver Eagle coin only has a face value of $1! So for example, since American Silver Eagles have a face value of $1, you

75

could maybe get away with taking 9,999 Silver Eagles out of the country legally. As of this writing, you still might be able to depending on the mood and/or intelligence of your TSA or customs agent. But this little loophole could have recently changed or at the very least, could be open to interpretation. I can't seem to get a straight answer from US Customs or the TSA but the rules on the US Customs and Border Protection website state:

"There is no duty on gold coins, medals or bullion but these items must be declared to a Customs and Border Protection (CBP) Officer. Please note a FinCEN 105 form must be completed at the time of entry for monetary instruments over $10,000. This includes currency, ie. gold coins, valued over $10,000. The FINCEN definition of currency: The coin and paper money of the United States or any other country that is (1) designated as legal tender and that (2) circulates and (3) is customarily accepted as a medium of exchange in the country of issuance. If you have doubt whether your gold/gold coin is considered a monetary instrument it is in your best interest to declare the item(s) with a CBP Officer, so you do not give a false declaration."

So are you supposed to value gold and silver using the face value of the coin or current spot price of the metal? Are your gold and silver coins currency or monetary instruments? In my opinion, they leave you asking this question on purpose. There is a great book called "Three Felonies A Day: How the Feds Target the Innocent" in which the author, civil liberties lawyer Harvey Silverglate, illustrates how modern federal laws are intentionally kept broad and vague in order to be able to prosecute you at anytime if you do something that displeases "the state." Very 1984-ish. Under these laws, the typical American probably commits a few felonies a day.

That being said, it isn't illegal to come or go with more than $10,000 of precious metals though. If you do want to carry more than $10,000 in precious metals you may have to declare and fill out the Financial Crimes Enforcement Network (FinCen) 105 form.

Keeping in mind the "three felonies a day theory," there may also be a rule you need to pay attention to from the US Census Bureau which requires you to make a declaration if the value of specific commodities that you're exporting are worth more than $2,500; in which case you would need to fill out a "Shippers Export Declaration" form. There may be a loophole for avoiding this rule called the "baggage and personal effects" exemption but, it seems everything is designed to be able to find you at fault if the government chooses to do so.

Now, if you're going to be traveling through other countries, you've got to be very careful when going through their customs. Make sure to know all the import/export rules of all the countries you're passing through. Even if you do know the rules, you never know when you'll run into a customs agent who knows your $50 gold American Eagle is really worth $1400 and decides he wants to levy his own "tax" on you.

In order to avoid having your metals stolen along the way from crooked customs agents, you could travel with small .23oz British Sovereigns or .18oz gold coins from Germany, Switzerland or France. These coins are not only gold, but they have collectible value as well and easily pass for simple pocket change when you walk through x-ray machines at borders or airports. Some precious metals dealers are starting to sell gold bullion jewelry, like necklaces or bracelets that allow you to wear a couple ounces of gold bullion across borders.

I'll take small amounts with me occasionally, but besides the small coins I've mentioned, I really don't travel with precious metals internationally. It's just too much of a risk.

If you are planning on moving a large amount of metal out of the country on your own, I would lessen the risk by taking multiple trips with smaller amounts of metals; or at least do a couple test runs with smaller amounts to get an idea of any obstacles you may face when moving a larger amount of precious metal. I would also consider seeing if you can get them insured against loss or confiscation. In most cases, the smartest thing to do when trying to transport a large dollar amount of gold or silver is to use a professional transport company like Brinks Global Services or any of the others I mention in the resource section of this book. Doing this allows your metals to be fully secured, insured and all their paperwork and customs clearances are taken care of in advance.

If you must travel and leave the USA with gold and silver in your bag, the safest way to transport your metals is to, unfortunately, declare them using their current market value instead of their face value and fill out the Financial Crimes Enforcement Network (FinCen) 105 form. Make sure to check the customs rules of the country you are traveling to.

One more question I get asked a lot is if I bring gold and silver into the United States? Well, if I did bring precious metals into the USA, I would declare them and fill out the FinCen form 105 but usually I just answer these questions by telling the questioner that I am not insane. Once I get metal out of the USA, I keep it out of the USA.

Chapter 11

HOW DO I SELL MY GOLD AND SILVER?

Yes, I know the subtitle of this book is "How to Buy Gold and Silver Bullion Without Getting Ripped Off!" but in this chapter I'm going to give you my thoughts on how to sell your metal.

Selling is the easy part. If you follow the advice in this book, you can sell your precious metals back for cash to the custodian who is storing your metal, which is also most likely the dealer you originally bought your metal from. Once sold, they'll wire the cash directly to your bank account in a couple days average or mail you a check. When you buy some metal from an online dealer and set up your account, you'll see how easy this is. It's probably a good idea to test out how well this works and sell a small amount back to your dealer to see how efficient their system is. If you have physical metals in your possession, you can walk down to your local coin shop and sell some of your metal or even list it on a website like Craigslist (make sure to meet the buyer in a safe spot like a police station parking lot).

Tax Saving Sales Strategy

Before trying this strategy, make sure to consult with

your CPA and tax attorney. There is a term in stock investing known as a "wash sale." Normally you don't get to deduct your losses if you sell your stock at a loss and then buy that same stock back within thirty days. However, wash sale rules currently do not apply to gold and silver bullion. Here's how it works.

You sell your gold and silver bullion for less than you paid for it (a loss). A few days later you buy back the gold and silver you sold. When you do this, you get to treat the loss on your tax return as a capital loss that can offset your gains from stocks or real estate etc. Even better, that loss can carry over year after year forever until you have gains to use it against! Your dealer needs to actually take title of the gold and silver you sell and give you the cash as well as issue a receipt. Run this little gem of a strategy by your tax attorney and CPA for full details.

Random Thoughts on Selling Your Metals

Sometimes if there's a big spike in gold or silver prices I will put in a sell order for my ETFs or buy some put options. But I'm saving up my physical metals for the day when the gold and silver markets absolutely skyrocket. You'll know when that day comes because everyone and their mothers will be talking about gold and silver. It will be total madness. Like the dot-com/tech stock bubble in 2000. Go to the library and check out the book "Extraordinary Popular Delusions and the Madness of Crowds" by Charles Mackay. He talks about financial manias and bubbles throughout history like the Dutch Tulip mania in the 17th century and the South Sea bubble.

As you can probably guess, I really never sell my stack of physical gold and silver. Until the crazy days I mentioned above come, or until I absolutely need to cash out for emergency reasons, I'll keep stacking. If I am convinced that gold or silver may be trending down, I will sometime hedge my physical position buying an inverse ETF designed to make money when gold or silver goes down in price. If I feel convinced that silver is going down in the near term I'll sometimes buy the ProShares UltraShort Silver ETF (ZSL). If I think gold is headed south for a bit I might buy ProShares Ultra Short Gold ETF (GLL). Be careful though! If you're wrong and the metal moves the other way you'll lose money.

Also keep in mind that gold is very similar to a currency but not necessarily looked at in the same way. So you've got to be careful when assessing its relative strength, weakness or value. For instance, when the US dollar gets stronger, it can look like the value of gold goes down. But just viewing gold in this light doesn't give you the bigger picture of how valuable gold is in the rest of the world because an increase in the price of gold could be due to a change in the value of the dollar. You can compare the price of gold in relation to other foreign currencies to get a handle on its overall value. Keep an eye on the Kitco Gold Index (KGX) for a better idea of gold's real value. It will show you the actual value of gold and how much the price of gold currently reflects a change in the price of the dollar.

Selling Your Silver In Europe

If you transport or sell your silver in Europe, you're getting ripped off in my opinion. For some reason, the

Europeans seem very prejudiced against silver bullion. As of this writing, many countries in the European Union charge a value added tax (VAT) when you buy, sell, take delivery of or even transport your silver holdings. I believe Estonia may be the only European country with no VAT on silver. This VAT can be as high as almost 30% in some countries. There is no VAT tax for gold bullion. The rules are all over the place and taxes can vary for each country or even depending on the type of silver you are buying or selling so make sure to be aware and do you due diligence before buying or selling silver in the European Union.

Chapter 12

WHAT ABOUT TAXES, REPORTING AND PRIVACY?

What about taxes? First off, I'm not an attorney and this is not legal advice. Make sure to consult with your tax attorney and CPA when dealing with your precious metals and taxes and any of the following is subject to change. Do your due diligence. One more thing before we get into this, all of these idiotic rules are courtesy of the Bank Secrecy Act of 1970 and the 2001 Patriot Act.

Is selling and buying gold and silver a private transaction or is it reported to the Internal Revenue Service?

There are two reporting requirements that dealers follow when you buy or sell precious metals. As you probably know, when you buy gold and silver there is nothing to fill out and it's basically a private transaction unless you're buying $10,000 or more of gold and silver using cash or cash equivalents or using cash in a series of related buying transactions that add up to $10,000 or more in less than a 24-hour period. In this case, the dealer will have to file IRS form 8300 and a Suspicious Activity Report, also known as a "SAR," with the Financial Crimes Enforcement Network. The IRS defines cash as not only cash (currency or bills) but also any cashier's check, money orders, bank drafts or traveler's checks that have a face value of $10,000 or less. For example, if you go to a dealer and buy $13,000 worth of Gold Eagles and use a personal check or credit card, the buy is not reportable and there are no IRS forms to fill out. If you were to pay in hundred dollar bills, then the dealer would be required to fill out IRS form 8300. If you bought $9,999 worth of Gold Eagles and paid in cash, the dealer would not be required to fill out any IRS form. The vast majority of precious metal buys do not require reporting.

Now when you sell your precious metals back to your custodian or dealer, some transactions are private and some are not private which means the dealer must report them. Make sure you consult with your tax attorney first. Sometimes a dealer will have to fill out an IRS form 1099-B. This depends on what type of gold and silver you are selling and in what dollar amount. As of this writing, various American Gold Eagle coins and American Gold Buffalo coins are exempt from 1099 reporting. Canadian Silver Maple Leaf coins, Austrian Philharmonic silver coins and American Silver Eagle coins are also exempt from IRS form 1099-B reporting.

Your dealer has to fill out IRS form 1099-B when you sell 1,000 ounces or more in silver rounds or bars as well as $1000 or more in face value of junk silver. They must also fill out IRS form 1099-B when you sell one kilo (31.15 troy ounces) or more of gold bars per transaction or twenty-five ounces or more of foreign gold coins.

What about taxes?

In the United States, whether your sale required dealer reporting or not, if you sell your metals for a profit, this means you have a taxable gain and you have to pay taxes on that gain which are called "capital gains taxes." The IRS treats all precious metals as "collectibles" for income tax protocol. Any gains you make on your "collectibles" that you hold for less than one year are taxed as ordinary income and treated as short term capital gains. Any gains you make on your "collectibles" that you hold for more than one year are treated as long term and taxed at a maximum rate of 28%. This goes for physical precious metals, numismatic coins and paper precious metals like ETFs!

Is there any required reporting for foreign held precious metals?

If you open a foreign bank account, brokerage or gold depository account with a financial institution, you need to fill out the FinCEN form 114, also known as the FBAR (Foreign Bank and Financial Accounts Report). FinCEN is the US Treasury's Financial Crimes Enforcement Network. You can learn more about this reporting requirement here: www.stacksilvergetgold.com/fbar

More rules to be aware of are the reporting requirements of the Foreign Account Tax Compliance Act, also known as FACTA, IRS form 8938. As of this writing, this rule is rather murky when it comes to gold depository accounts overseas.

Right now, it seems that if you store your precious metals in a private, foreign, non-bank vault or safe deposit box that does not charge you "fabrication fees" when you take your gold out of storage, it is not required to be reported since the business storing your metals is not considered a financial institution and the non-bank safe deposit box or vault holding your metals is not considered a financial account. To be safe, make sure to double check with the IRS and ask a lawyer for up-to-date expert guidance. Evading government reporting requirements is one of the fastest ways to "get ripped off" and lose all your gold and silver. You can see what the IRS has to say about the difference between FBAR and FACTA reporting here:

www.stacksilvergetgold.com/fbar8938

Recently, the IRS answered many questions on reporting precious metals stored offshore and form 8938 that could confirm, in my opinion, holding gold directly in a private, foreign non-bank vault or safe deposit box is not reportable. Here are two of the answered IRS questions taken directly from the IRS website.

> **Q:** *I directly hold precious metals for investment, such as gold, in a foreign country. Do I need to report these assets on Form 8938?*

> **A:** *No. Directly held precious metals, such as gold, are not specified foreign financial assets. Note, however, that gold certificates issued by a foreign person may be a specified foreign financial asset that you would have to report on Form 8938, if the total value of all your specified foreign financial assets is greater than the reporting threshold that applies to you.*

> **Q:** *I have a safe deposit box at a foreign financial institution. Is the safe deposit box itself considered to a financial account?*

> **A:** *No, a safe deposit box is not a financial account.*

You can find the above answers and how the IRS answers many more reporting related questions here: www.stacksilvergetgold.com/8938IRS

I know. Lots of rules. Don't just rely on this book since the rules could change at any time. Talk to your CPA and tax attorney about buying, selling and reporting precious metals and show them the two IRS links above.

Chapter 13

HOW ARE YOU PERSONALLY INVESTING IN GOLD AND SILVER?

Gold and silver are commodities. Every single precious metals dealer or broker is selling the exact same thing; no one has any magic gold or silver out there. Buy from an honest dealer with relatively low premiums (not necessarily the lowest) and a solid reputation. Don't get persuaded into paying more because the coin is a mint condition this or that.

The company at www.stacksilvergetgold.com/ownx happens to be my favorite for gold and silver investing and the one I recommend and use the most.

What's great about this American dealer custodian is that for beginning and smaller to medium-sized investors, they allow you to start a gold and silver investing program with a low minimum purchase of just $25 and include special fully insured, allocated and un-segregated private vault storage. They also allow larger investors to make sizable purchases of $100,000 or higher if that's what you're looking for. You can choose to make a one-time purchase, or you can do what I do and automate your gold and silver investing.

To automate your investing, you set up a monthly or weekly gold and silver investing account in which each month or week, a certain amount of money that you choose is deducted from your bank account and used to buy physical gold or silver bullion on the open market where it is then transferred to a fully insured, allocated and un-segregated private vault storage facility. By investing this way, you "dollar cost average" and slowly accumulate a large amount of silver and gold bullion over time.

When you "dollar cost average" into gold and silver, you are making same dollar amount investments at regular time intervals and you end up buying more gold and silver when it is cheaper, and less when it is more expensive. This will turn you into a disciplined precious metals investor instead of an undisciplined trader who buys or sells on emotion. When you gain this investor mentality, you'll be happy to see the prices for gold or silver dip because that means a better buying opportunity for you. You get more metal for your money. I use this monthly investing program as do many of my friends and family. It's a wise way to build discipline into your gold and silver investing and stack up a nice amount of precious metals.

Once you have saved up at least twenty ounces of silver or one ounce of gold, you can have your silver delivered to your home at any time in one ounce coins or rounds, ten ounce bars, one hundred ounce bars, junk silver bags or even one thousand ounce bars. Your can have your gold delivered in kilo bars or one ounce coins. Watch this video to see me receiving and opening up an OWNx delivery of silver bars and gold coins: www.stacksilvergetgold.com/silverdelivery

Their premium and storage fees are also very reasonable, well within my required range. This is a smart and honest dealer and the first place I suggest for anyone who wants to buy gold and silver bullion. Because silver is relatively cheaper than gold at the moment, you can compile a war chest of silver in no time. As for gold, they allow you to start buying it by the grain if you would like; a grain of gold at the moment currently costs only about two and a half dollars! You can find out more and set up your own account here:

www.stacksilvergetgold.com/ownx

By the way, I have a small portion of my gold and silver from this custodian delivered to my home and I keep it in my safe. The majority of it I just leave in their private vault storage. I tend to use fully-insured, allocated, and un-segregated storage instead of segregated storage whenever possible because it is a bit cheaper in terms of storage fees.

If the price of gold or silver dips significantly, sometimes I walk on over to my local coin shop and buy some physical gold or silver. This is fine to do as long as you find a dealer that charges a reasonable premium.

Gold tends to be seasonal in nature like many commodities. Its price can fluctuate due to the same repeating reasons year after year. Wedding season in India is an example of one of these reasons. Going back to 1975, statistics show that the best performing months for gold have been September, October and January. March has been the only month where gold has been down in every kind of market condition! Gold has been down in March in bull markets, bear markets and sideways markets. So if you're going to make a huge gold buy, it might be a good idea to wait until March but, otherwise, just start stacking now - at least a little bit!

I usually check the "for sale" listings on Craigslist.com every once in a while. You can often buy ten or one hundred ounce silver bars at whatever the day's spot price is, with no premium! Stick to the larger bars because they are much harder to fake than rounds. I avoid buying off of eBay due to the counterfeit horror stories I've heard and how people can create fake accounts to bid up the price of the metals they are selling. I've been buying bars off of Craigslist for many years and have never once seen a fake but that doesn't mean they don't exist so you still have to be careful. If you buy coins on Craigslist, try to buy the American Gold and Silver Eagles. There is a huge penalty in the USA for counterfeiting these coins. Avoid anything from China as they are counterfeiting like crazy over there. Here is a good YouTube video on how to spot fake silver:
www.stacksilvergetgold.com/spotfakegoldsilver

Chapter 14

DO YOU LIKE GOLD OR SILVER BETTER?

I personally buy more silver than gold. That being said, I think there's a bit more risk involved with silver and it tends to be more volatile than gold but the potential rewards are worth it in my opinion. Don't get me wrong, I still love gold and I am buying it up like a maniac. I'm just buying more silver; probably 60% silver and 40% gold. Here are some of my reasons for buying gold and silver.

There isn't that much silver left in the world

According to a United States geological survey and many silver experts, at current mining rates, the world will run out of silver in about twenty years. Even more shocking is that if all mining were to stop, the current above ground amount of silver would only last about four months. Gold is in a similar position. When there is high demand and low supply, the price has no choice but to rise. I want to have a big war chest of gold and silver stacked up before my barber starts talking to me about how much money he made selling his mothers jewelry to one of those "we buy gold" places.

For example, let's use the metal Palladium. Palladium is

a silver-like metal that used to trade for about $100 an ounce. When the industrial demand rose and supply shrunk, it shot up to over $1000 an ounce and has stayed in a higher dollar trading range ever since. Silver is even better because it has both industrial demand and investor demand whereas palladium really only has industrial demand. So when silver supplies start to shrink and demand rises, watch out!

Silver has huge industrial demand

Silver is used for batteries, solar energy, water filters, coins, electrical, electronics, mirrors, photography, catalysts, coatings, wood preservatives, bearings, electroplating, brazing, soldering, jewelry, medical applications, silverware and more. Industry and photography combine to make up about 65% of the total demand for silver. Much of the silver used to make things like computers, microwaves, refrigerators or cell phones can't be replaced or recycled after use! This means that silver is being used at maddening rates. So if the world heats up instead of getting depressed, there's more upside to silver because industrial demand in many countries will increase. The majority of gold is used strictly for investment purposes and jewelry although it is also used in some industries like biotech.

Silver could go through the roof when the public eventually jumps on the bandwagon, or it could go through the roof just for the simple fact that we are running out of it. The less there is of something, means the more value it holds.

The public is ALWAYS late to the party!

Gold fever will most likely hit first and the price of gold will take off. The future is bright and shiny if you're a gold investor. However, this is also great news for silver investors because the general public will jump on the gold bandwagon first. As the price of gold rises and becomes too expensive for the average investor to buy, where do you think people are going to turn to? That's right, silver! Poor man's gold. Get in when everyone else is getting in and you're probably too late. The smart money gets in when the asset is undervalued like silver is today.

The Government is "Depressing"

Fifty years ago, almost every single government in the world had huge stockpiles of silver and gold. The United States alone had about 3.5 billion ounces of silver. Since then, all of the governments have been selling their silver. This massive selling has put an artificial, downward pressure on the price of silver. In other words, it has kept the price of silver low. The cool thing is that in 2007, most governments stopped their selling because they ran out of silver.

Today, the world's governments control only about 60 million ounces of silver. The United States has only about 20 million ounces left, and that was from a high of 3.5 billion ounces! In fact, the US Mint now has to go on the open market to buy silver to mint its Silver Eagle coins. The hangover from this tremendous amount of selling is ending. Around 2009, central banks became net buyers of gold for the first time in decades. Not only are governments, like China and

Russia for instance, becoming huge buyers of gold and silver but they are even encouraging their citizens to own precious metals.

So where did all the silver the governments sold go?

I know what you're thinking. If governments sold all this silver, someone must have bought it and is still holding onto it, right? Well, the huge industrial manufacturers bought it and then they used it to make stuff for us! You know about silver's uses now so here's a crucial point. Silver has tons of uses while gold has two main uses, money and jewelry. Ninety percent of the gold ever produced in the history of the world is still in existence and available. Silver, since it gets used up for things like batteries and water purification, is getting depleted at a faster rate than gold.

For the first time in history, silver is now more rare than gold! When the general public, major investment houses and the world's governments catch on to silver again, it should explode in value. And just wait until the middle classes in China and India start buying cell phones and refrigerators and computers the way we do in America.

Is the price of silver being manipulated?

The price of silver is regularly manipulated. In 2016, Deutsche Bank paid 38 million dollars in fines to settle a lawsuit for silver market rigging. As part of the deal, they had to release hundreds of thousands of private emails and documents. In these emails, you find clear evidence of silver market rigging from not just Deutsche Bank but from HSBC Holdings Plc, UBS Group AG, the Bank of Nova Scotia and more firms.

Big banks acting like scumbags don't usually benefit you, but sometimes they do…let me explain. About four major traders regularly use the New York Commodities and Mercantile Exchange to sell a heck of a lot of silver. There's only one issue, the silver that these guys sell doesn't exist! They sell it in the form of silver futures contracts.

Futures contracts are just pieces of paper stating that the seller will provide you with the amount of silver sold at some point in the future. Get this - these traders routinely sell double the amount of silver known to exist on earth. There is no other commodity with such an enormous short position. Only about 2% of existing gold is being sold in futures contracts, compared to 200% of silver!

Many silver experts now believe these entities are doing their best to keep the price of silver artificially low. This is excellent news for you because it means you can buy silver at a very cheap price right now. Those enormous short positions in the futures markets are keeping the price of physical silver low. One day, when we start running out of physical silver and the public gets into it as well, these traders will not be able to hold the price down artificially in the futures markets; they will be caught in what is known as a "short squeeze" and the real price of silver will soar. There is a similar, but not as extreme, situation happening to gold as well. For more on how this happens you may want to check out the Gold Anti

Trust Action Committee website at www.gata.org

The big boys are beginning to catch on

So the governments, the public and major investment houses haven't really caught on yet, but the big boys with the smart money certainly have. The world's richest men, billionaires like Warren Buffet, George Soros, Bill Gates and Lawrence Tish, have all been buying silver. They see that silver is close to an all time low when adjusted for inflation. Forbes Magazine has shown that the real value of silver for hundreds of years when adjusted for inflation has been between $100-200 an ounce.

Oh, and one more thing, it looks like the governments of Russia, China and India are becoming big buyers as well. They buy tons of gold too. In fact, many foreign central banks are starting to stockpile gold again and may soon start stockpiling silver. Germany has even asked the United States to send all of its gold back to them! What does this tell you? It tells me Germany doesn't trust the US government with its money anymore and reinforces the fact that you definitely want to have some of your gold and silver in your physical possession.

Silver outperforms gold in bull markets

Historically, when there's been a precious metals bull market, silver has outperformed gold for the most part. According to analysts, about 1% of the world is invested in gold. Only .02% is invested in silver. So, it's going to take less people getting interested in silver to make a significant upward move in the market. Silver is also called the "poor man's gold," since the average person can afford to buy some silver.

Then there is the gold to silver ratio. The gold/silver ratio is the amount of silver it takes to buy one ounce of gold. To calculate the gold/silver ratio, all you have to do is take the current price of gold and divide it by the current price of silver. For thousands of years, the gold to silver ratio averaged around fifteen ounces of silver to one ounce of gold or 15:1. As of this writing in 2017, the gold/silver ratio is around 70:1. This means that silver has a lot of appreciating to do in order to get back to that historical ratio average. Another way of saying it is that silver at the moment is historically cheap when compared to gold. Now if the ratio was 10:1 for example, that would mean that gold was historically cheap compared to silver.

As a brief aside, now that you know what the gold to silver ratio is, I'd like to tell you about the gold to silver ratio trade. For the last few decades, the gold to silver ratio has fluctuated from about 85:1 on the high end to 40:1 on the low end. The gold to silver ratio trade consists of selling silver when the gold/silver ratio drops below 45:1 and buying gold with the proceeds. When the gold/silver ratio then gets to 80:1 or above, you sell your gold and buy silver. In other words, you're buying gold or silver when they are relatively cheap in terms of each other. Over the last few decades this trade has made some big profits. You can see the current gold to silver ratio here: www.stacksilvergetgold.com/goldsilverratio

If you're looking for a ratio to tell you when it may be a good time to buy gold, you can check out the Dow to

Gold ratio which is the ratio of the Dow Jones Industrial Average to the price of gold. This ratio tells you how many ounces of gold it would take to buy the Dow at any given time. As of this writing the Dow to gold ratio is about 17:1 and, historically speaking, this means gold is relatively cheap compared to the DJIA. You can see the current Dow to Gold ratio here: www.stacksilvergetgold.com/dowgold

The Federal Reserve

This may seem out of left field, but you need to know it because the Federal Reserve creates inflation and inflation makes the value of the dollar go down and the prices of silver and gold go up. The Federal Reserve is not really a US Government agency. It is basically a privately owned bank that also pays dividends to private stockholders! Amazing, right? Some of the world's largest banks "own" the Federal Reserve; not the United States Government. The US Congress has granted the Federal Reserve the right to create dollars out of thin air and this is how inflation happens. Inflation is an increase in the money supply. Higher prices of goods are a symptom of inflation. The Federal Reserve is not audited and not accountable to Congress.

A long time ago, you could exchange one dollar for a set amount of gold. This was called "the gold standard." We eventually had to go off the gold standard because the Federal Reserve was printing too much money and the US treasury didn't have enough gold to back up all those extra dollars that were printed. When the USA went off the gold standard, it gave the Federal Reserve free reign to print as much "funny money" as it wanted to. Once people begin to realize a currency is becoming "funny money" (like the dollar may be now), they usually start paying attention to gold and silver because they are a real store of value that can't be printed or created with just a number entry on a computer. Inflating currency to pay for wars and social programs has happened many times throughout history and it has always ended in disaster for the currency that was inflated. Every single fiat (paper) currency has always become worthless. There is a fantastic book on the history and origins of the Federal Reserve called The Creature From Jekyll Island. Definitely worth reading!

Chapter 15

HOW CAN I GET SILVER FOR FREE FROM BANKS?

Well, not exactly for free. You can actually get silver bullion for the price of the face value of the particular coin. Earlier in this book I told you about "junk silver." Junk silver refers to dimes, nickels, quarters, half dollars and dollars that were made in the United States before 1965. Most of these junk silver coins contain about 90% real silver.

It's rare that you find junk silver in your pocket change today. Most pre-1965 coins have been filtered out of circulation by banks and collectors over time, but you still can find some every once in a while so make a habit of checking your change anyway. However, there is a little loophole with junk silver that some banks don't seem to know.

The secret lies with the Kennedy half dollar. Silver was taken out of all coins in 1965 except for the Kennedy half dollar. The Kennedy half dollar contained 40% silver from 1965 to 1970. Hundreds of millions of these coins were minted. Many people collected these coins and the fact that they contain silver is not widely known.

Some banks still have rolls of these Kennedy half

dollars in their vaults. So the trick is, any time you're near or walk in a bank, ask them for a few rolls of half dollars. This doesn't work all the time. It doesn't even work the majority of the time, but it does work sometimes.

You really can't lose any money trying. You give the bank $30 and they give you the equivalent face value of half dollars. If that roll of half dollars contains 1965-1970 Kennedy half dollars, you just got a lot of silver for way under the spot price. You may even get lucky and find some older half dollars as well! By the way, you can check the silver content of any coin by visiting a website called Coinflation at:
www.stacksilvergetgold.com/coinflation

SUGGESTED RESOURCES:

The following are my "go-to" resources for all things related to investing in gold and silver bullion. I've read each book I've recommended multiple times and I've bought gold and silver from each dealer I recommend. I've also tested out any products I suggest, like the book safe! The only resources that I haven't personally used are some of the private storage companies and the IRA custodians. In this case, I first learned about the company because it was a favorite of another expert whom I trust in the industry. I've researched each of these companies and selected what I thought were the best of the best. The latest updates to this resource section can be found at:
 www.stacksilvergetgold.com/resources

BEST BOOK RECOMMENDATIONS

"Rich Dad's Advisor Series: Guide to Investing in Gold and Silver: Protect Your Financial Future" by Michael Maloney

This is one of the best books on gold and silver investing available and was recently updated in 2015. Just by reading this one book, you'll probably know more about gold and silver investing and why you should invest in gold and silver than most professional traders. Get this one for sure. In fact, most of the "Rich

Dad Series" books are all pretty good. Stack Silver Get Gold is more to the point; this book goes deeper into history and the reasons why you should be buying gold and silver. It's a competitor to my book for sure, but a worthy competitor.
www.stacksilvergetgold.com/michaelmaloney

"The Collapse of the Dollar and How to Profit from It" by James Turk and John Rubino

This is another great book that explains the current situation of the economy and why the authors believe the dollar will eventually collapse. It then tells you how to invest your money wisely so that you can profit from that collapse. Guess what their number one recommendation is? Gold and silver. The history of gold and silver is also expertly explained. One of my favorite parts of this book is that it gives you a very good primer, if you're interested, on how to get into gold and silver mining stocks. More info at: www.stacksilvergetgold.com/collapse

"The Creature from Jekyll Island" by G. Edward Griffin

G. Edward Griffin's book isn't about gold and silver investing, but it does explain how our economic and financial system works and reviews how financial systems evolved throughout history. Once you understand the big picture of how our financial system works, you can then make the connection to the importance of gold and silver investing. This may be the most interesting and most profitable book you will ever read. By the way, "The Creature from Jekyll Island" refers to the secret meeting of bankers and the creation of the Federal Reserve in 1913 on Jekyll Island in Georgia. This book is a must read. Get more info at www.stacksilvergetgold.com/jekyll

"The Dollar Crisis: Causes, Consequences, Cures" by Richard Duncan

This is the book that opened my eyes to what's going on within the United States economy and got me seriously investing in gold and silver. Richard reveals what is wrong with the world's monetary system. He also examines the United States trade deficit and evolving credit bubbles and gives you a road map for surviving the future. Duncan has also written "The New Depression" and "The Corruption of Capitalism". Find out more at www.stacksilvergetgold.com/richardduncan

"Economics in One Lesson: The Smartest and Surest Way to Understand Basic Economics" by Henry Hazlitt

This isn't one of those books that are required for knowing how to invest in gold and silver and you certainly don't have to run out and buy it now but this is a very important book nonetheless. It gives you an insightful overview of general economics and then breaks down the major economic fallacies. It puts you on sound economic ground so that politicians can't take advantage of you. A brilliant book. Buy it. Read it. Many times. www.stacksilvergetgold.com/henryhazlitt

WHERE TO BUY GOLD AND SILVER ONLINE

The following are my favorite "one stop shop" companies where I buy most of my metals from. Are there other reputable places to buy from online? Yes. But they are few and far between. You don't want to take the chance of buying from a dealer just because they offer you the lowest price. That's a good way to get ripped off. Remember what we talked about earlier in the gold and silver scams section? I've selected and used these guys because of their honest reputation, good reviews, the ease of buying and the full service they provide. With the recommendations below, you can make a onetime purchase and ship your metals to your house. You can buy gold and silver bullion and then have them store it for you in fully insured and secured private vault storage. And since they are custodians, they can also sell your metals on your behalf whenever you ask them to. This is where I recommend you start.

OWNx

This is my favorite gold and silver dealer and custodian in the United States and the custodial dealer I personally use the most, as well as suggest to the majority of people who ask me who they should buy their metals through. They have an A+ rating with the Better Business Bureau and tons of great reviews. Founded in 2008, OWNx is my preferred way for beginning investors to start buying gold or silver bullion since the minimum purchase that will get you full access to all their precious metals investing tools is only $25. If you're a whale, they'll also let you make purchases well over $100,000.

The silver and gold bullion you buy is allocated and titled in your name, it's insured 100% and stored at the private high security First State Depository vault located in Wilmington, Delaware. Their allocated, un-segregated storage is smart if you're just starting out because it means you pay less in storage fees and have more money left over to buy your metal with. If it's an emergency and you need to sell, you can do that instantly through your 24/7 account dashboard and your cash will be wired to your bank account in a business day.

You can also make a one-time purchase or choose to have your silver and gold delivered to you at any time which I routinely do. They can ship you a wide variety of metal including American Gold and Silver Eagles, Austrian Philharmonics, Krugerrands, British Sovereigns, bags of junk silver, kilo gold bars, and silver bars ranging from one ounce to one thousand ounces all of which you can select through your account dashboard. They have recently added the option to set up a precious metals IRA directly through your account too which makes the process of creating a precious metals IRA much easier.

My favorite part is their automated precious metals investing program. To me, the most important thing is to make gold and silver investing a habit. Using their automated program is like instantly installing a precious metals investing habit into your life. It's a very simple process. You select the amount of gold and/or silver you'd like to purchase every month and OWNx automates the process for you and makes the purchase on your behalf each month, allowing you to take advantage of "dollar cost averaging" that I mentioned earlier in the book. You can increase or decrease the amount at any time or stop the purchases altogether. But I have never stopped since I started. No matter what else is happening in my life or distracting me, my gold and silver stacking is on autopilot thanks to this program. My friends, members of my family and I use their automated investing program and buy gold and silver every month on a consistent, set it and forget it basis. Start your OWNx account now or learn more about their program here: www.stacksilvergetgold.com/ownx

Bullion Vault

Bullion Vault is kind of like the OWNx of Europe so it's a great place to start stacking if you live in Europe and a it's good spot to internationalize your gold if you already have something set up in the United States. This company was founded in 2005 and houses more than two billion dollars of gold bullion for over sixty-five thousand customers. Bullion Vault is a full member of the London Bullion Market Association and can buy and sell your metals on your behalf.

Although it is headquartered in London, they offer allocated gold and silver bullion stored in your choice of vaults located in London, Zurich, Toronto, New York City and Singapore. The vaults are operated by Brinks and Via Mat International. Their low fees are possible because they only buy "good delivery" bars. These are the same bars that central banks, investment funds and mints trade and use. The gold bars are 400 ounces and the silver bars are 1000 ounces. When you make a metals purchase you are essentially buying a specific amount or weight of one bar. You can have your gold delivered to you in amounts of 50 grams or more. However they will only deliver your silver to you in 1000 ounce bars and, since this is a UK registered company, your silver withdrawals will also be subject to a VAT tax. Because of this, I don't recommend you use Bullion Vault if you are looking to get silver delivered to your home. There is no VAT tax applied to gold withdrawals.

If you'd like to sell your metals holdings, they will make the sale for you and transfer the money into your bank account usually within a business day or two. So when you set up an account with these guys, you're really setting it up for the overseas storage and accumulation; not home delivery. To set up an account you need a valid ID, proof of address, a bank statement and a money transfer from your bank account to your Bullion Vault account. Like OWNx, it is free to set up and keep an ongoing account. They also have an automated investing program which will allow you to dollar cost average into gold. You pay reasonable prices for monthly insured storage fees and gold or silver transactions. You can see a review and set up your account at www.stacksilvergetgold.com/bullionvault

Miles Franklin

If you're looking to make a huge precious metals purchase, *I'm talking hundreds of thousands to millions of dollars*, you go to Miles Franklin. Based in Minnesota, Miles Franklin has been in business almost 30 years has an A+ rating with the Better Business Bureau. It is one of only 24 dealers in the world approved and authorized as a US Mint reseller. It's crazy but the precious metals industry is not federally regulated. But if you set up shop in Minnesota, like Miles Franklin purposely did, you are regulated by the state. These guys are licensed, bonded and every broker must pass a full background check. Due to state regulations, they can only allow online purchases of up to $5,000 from their website. Anything over $5,000 and you have to work directly with one of their brokers. I highly recommend doing this. Most of their brokers have been in the precious metals industry for a decade or more and know their stuff. As you'll see below, they can set up foreign vault storage or a safe deposit box for you as well. You can schedule a consultation with me and I'll introduce you to my personal broker or their founder, Andy Schectman. Andy also has a personal 1-800 number that you can dial up at 1-800-255-1129 or you can just set up an online account directly from their website at: www.stacksilvergetgold.com/milesfranklin

PRIVATE VAULTS AND SAFETY DEPOSIT BOXES (FOREIGN AND DOMESTIC)

Here are some of the world's best private vaults and storage companies. Besides the biggest players in highly secure vault storage which are Loomis, Brinks and Malca-Amit, I've found the facilities listed below to be top notch. Just tell them Hunter from Stack Silver Get Gold sent you and they'll treat you like gold. Man, that's a lame joke.

Delaware: First State Depository is the private vault storage company used by OWNx but you do not have

to be an OWNx client to store your precious metals at First State. These guys are one of the best in the country. They're fully insured by Lloyds of London. They offer super secure and segregated storage and they'll even come and pick up your metal in an armored car. Even better, First State doesn't trade, make markets or buy and sell inventory.
www.stacksilvergetgold.com/firststatedepository

Florida: For completely anonymous storage with no ID required, head to Sarasota, FL and check out the Sarasota Vault Depository. They have private safe deposit boxes and walk-in vaults. Sarasota Vault Depository will provide you with a Safe Keeping Receipt for your stored metals which you can then use for alternative financing if needed.
www.stacksilvergetgold.com/sarasotavaultdepository

Arizona: There's a private vault in Phoenix, Arizona that's embedded into the side of a mountain and surrounded by tons of steel, concrete and, well, mountain! The vault door weighs over 6000 pounds, they've got state of the art security systems and 24/7 armed guard security. So if you're not going to use OWNx and you already have a stack of silver and gold that you'd like to move to private storage, Mountain Vault is a rock solid choice.
www.stacksilvergetgold.com/mountainvault

Canada: One of the few dealers I trust and recommend in this book, Miles Franklin, also has an impenetrable private vault storage and safe deposit box program. Their vault storage is operated by Brinks Canada with locations in Toronto, Vancouver and Montreal. Your metal is fully segregated and insured and independently audited every year. You can place a precious metals order with Miles Franklin and have them added directly to their vault or you can drive in or ship in your metals as well. They also offer private, foreign safe deposit boxes! These safe deposit boxes are protected by Brinks, fully insured and are considered "non-bank" which means they currently do not have to be reported. The boxes come with only one key and you hold it so they cannot be opened by anyone but you. Prices start at $25 per month. Tell them Hunter from Stack Silver Get Gold sent you. www.stacksilvergetgold.com/milesfranklin

Singapore: Singapore is quickly becoming one of the gold and silver bullion storage centers of the world. It has very transparent rules and the country itself has low crime and corruption. You can buy gold and silver at almost any bank. Combine this with competitive storage prices and you've got a great option for storing your metals privately overseas. One of my favorite spots is called The Safe House. The Safe House is a fully insured, protected by armed security forces and private vault storage company. You can find more information on them at www.stacksilvergetgold. com/safehouse . You can also check out Certis CISCO, which is another non-bank storage and secure transport company that rents safe deposit boxes starting at $99 a year. www.stacksilvergetgold.com/certis

Switzerland: Historically speaking, if you want to store gold and silver bullion offshore, Switzerland is the place to do it. Their storage systems are very sophisticated and well-developed. The Swiss are world-renowned and simply one of the best in private wealth storage. If you've got a ton of precious metals to store, it is hard to beat the Swiss. Again, you want to find a private, non-bank storage center or vault. One of my favorite Swiss joints is located in Basel, Switzerland and called Casaforte Private Secure Storage. www.stacksilvergetgold.com/casaforte

Austria: Not only does this country make very cool gold and silver coins, the Austrian Philharmonic, they also love their metals, banking and secrecy in Austria. You can buy and sell gold and silver at just about every bank. Plus the Austrian government is in pretty good shape financially compared to the rest of Europe. As long as you show a photo ID you can get a safe deposit box at a bank like Bank Austria (www.bankaustria.at) and you can also buy gold from them VAT free. For totally anonymous and guarded private safety deposit box storage surrounded by more than one thousand tons of reinforced concrete, you want to head to the well-respected Das Safe in Vienna, Austria. Das Safe is so anonymous that once you pay for your safe, all they give you is the box key and a special pin code that will let you enter a secure room. You'll feel like you're in the movie The Da Vinci Code. Make sure you check out the opera house while you're in Vienna! www.stacksilvergetgold.com/dassafe

United Arab Emirates: Dubai and Abu Dhabi are the two cities where you want to head in the UAE. The UAE is the business and gold hub of the Middle East and very cooperative with the West. If you'd like to get a safe deposit box at a bank, I'd go to the Abu Dhabi Islamic Bank (www.adib.ae), one of the largest banks in the Middle East. They'll give you a safety deposit box if you show them a passport. You can find a fantastic

long-term secured vault storage service that's actually managed by Brinks Global Services at the Dubai Multi Commodities Centre in Dubai which is basically the commodity trading center of the UAE. Very safe and protected. Check them out at:
www.stacksilvergetgold.com/dmcc

Panama: If you're looking for a spot closer to the USA but still out of the country, Panama is a good option. Their government is very business friendly. The storage facility here is called Best Safety Boxes. It's a private joint right in the middle of the financial district. Prices start at about $350 per year. You can pay for your box for up to five years in advance. They seem to have a good security system in place with 24/7 armed forces. You can also add an insurance policy if you'd like. See them here:
www.stacksilvergetgold.com/bestsafetyboxes

PRECIOUS METALS TRANSPORT SERVICES

In the United States, shipping a small amount of metals is easy. You just have to make sure you insure whatever you ship and use a company like DHL, FedEx or UPS. But if you're moving a lot of metals in the United States, I suggest you use a professional, highly secure transport service like Brinks or IBI Armored Services. If you would like to ship your metals internationally, you can use Brinks Global, Malca-Amit, VIA MAT International or Emirate Airlines. Emirate Airlines has a "Protect-Premium" shipping service that includes video surveillance and secure service accompanied by armed security guards. Find out more at www.stacksilvergetgold.com/emirate

SELF-DIRECTED AND PRECIOUS METALS IRA CUSTODIANS

If you need help with setting up your self-directed or precious metals IRA here are some good options. Remember, only bullion in your IRAs!

The Entrust Group: These guys have been doing self-directed IRAs for over 30 years and have thousands of clients. They'll help you add precious metals to your IRA or set up a self-directed IRA. On their website, there's a great learning center with courses, articles and videos all about self-directed IRAs, their advantages and if they're right for you. Tell them Stack Silver Get Gold sent you.
www.stacksilvergetgold.com/entrustgroup

New Direction IRA, Inc: New Direction has partnered up with OWNx so you can easily set up a New Direction precious metals IRA directly through your OWNx account and dashboard. Once set up is complete, you accounts will be linked together and you can transfer gold and silver from your OWNx account to your New Direction IRA if you so desire. New Direction is in good standing with The Better Business Bureau and is FDIC insured.   www.stacksilvergetgold.com/newdirection

BRIGHT MINDS TO FOLLOW

In addition to the authors of the books I suggested earlier, the following cast of characters are people who have influenced and helped me in the gold and silver niche and with becoming a smarter investor in general. Very smart people. Many of these guys also sell gold and silver or have some sort of newsletter or investing service. I don't necessarily recommend everything they do and I'm sure they all aren't total infallible saints, not many of us are, but paying attention to these gentlemen will make sure your ship is heading in the right direction and help you to develop a metals mindset. Let's get into it.

Peter Schiff: I could have and probably should have included some of Peter's books in the recommended books section. He's written many brilliant books including "Crash Proof: How to Profit from the Coming Economic Collapse," "The Real Crash: America's Coming Bankruptcy" and "How an Economy Grows and Why It Crashes." Schiff, a very insightful economist, also has a regular radio show and podcast in which you'll learn about gold and silver and the economy in general. His insights are heavily influenced by the free market, Austrian School of Economics (something I suggest you become familiar with) and he correctly predicted the 2007 real estate bubble and 2008 financial crisis when the vast majority of people were blind to them. Very smart dude.
www.stacksilvergetgold.com/peterschiff

Doug Casey: The definitely not politically correct Doug Casey is an author, venture capitalist, investment advisor and libertarian philosopher. He's the founder of Casey Research which offers investment research, services and advice and also includes some of my favorite investment newsletters like "The International Speculator" which focuses on undervalued gold and silver mining stocks, explorers and discoveries. I also like the Casey Report for actionable intelligence on stocks, bonds, gold and silver, real estate, commodities and more. He offers lots of free advice which you can access by signing up for his email newsletters called The International Man and the Casey Daily Dispatch. www.stacksilvergetgold.com/dougcasey

Bill Bonner: Bonner is the founder of the 500 million dollar per year Agora publishing company and a great world thinker. He's written many books, one of my favorite being "Hormegeddon: How too Much of a Good Thing Leads to a Disaster." He also has a free email newsletter that I read almost daily called "Bill Bonner's Diary." Although he does touch on it from time to time, Bonner really doesn't talk about gold and silver all that much but I find he helps you develop the particular mindset that will lead you to realizing why buying gold and silver bullion is such a smart thing to do. He tells it like it is. www.stacksilvergetgold.com/billbonner

David Skarica: Although David isn't the most famous guy in this section, I definitely think he's one of the shrewdest in the entire gold and silver investing niche. As a student of Sir John Templeton, he's got a lot of experience because he started investing in precious metals at a very young age and he's written some good books including "The Great Supercycle" which covers market cycles, inflation and dollar devaluation. He runs his own newsletter called

"Addicted to Profits" and he's also partnered with Newsmax to launch a research newsletter called "The Gold Stock Advisor." David correctly called the real estate crash in 2007 and has also been frequently dead on when calling precious metals bull markets. He gives out a lot of free advice on his website but what I really like is the paid version where he shows you the exact moves he's making in metals. www.stacksilvergetgold.com/davidskarica

Eric Sprott: Sprott is a self-made billionaire who has said he has more than 90% of his wealth, except the shares in his Sprott Asset Management Company, invested in gold and silver! He also founded a precious metals dealer called Sprott Money. Oh, I almost forgot to mention, the Sprott Physical Gold Trust and Sprott Physical Silver Trust he founded which were set up as an alternative to some gold and silver ETFs that don't allow you to redeem your shares for actual gold or silver bullion. This guy lives and breathes gold and silver. Follow him and consider what he says carefully. www.stacksilvergetgol.com/ericsprott

Jim Rickards: Not only is Jim is one of the best minds to watch in metals today, he's also great for a macro view of where the world is heading since he's constantly traveling the globe and talking to insiders at ground zero of many different countries. Jim is an advisor on capital markets to the Secretary of Defense in the Pentagon and other US intelligence agencies. He is the author of many different best-sellers like "The Death of Money" and "Currency Wars." His most current book is called "The New Case for Gold". He is also the editor of a newsletter called "Strategic

Intelligence" which I read on a weekly basis. Find him at: www.stacksilvergetgold.com/rickards

The Dollar Vigilante: Warning! This guy isn't for everyone. He's pretty far out on the fringe compared to the other bright minds I have suggested so far and some of the speakers at his events are, in my opinion, a little nutty. The Dollar Vigilante considers himself a "Libertarian Anarcho-Capitalist" which basically means he's in favor of the elimination of the state and a return to individual sovereignty, private property, and free markets. When you follow The Dollar Vigilante, you'll learn about gold, silver and mining stocks but you'll also be first to know about other possible investments like cryptocurrencies. The Dollar Vigilante recommended buying bitcoin when it was only $3. Today bitcoin is trading around $1100. I'll put up with some nuttiness for discoveries like that! He has a low cost newsletter that I read regularly. Find it here: www.stacksilvergetgold.com/vigilante

Minesh Bhindi: Remember way back in the fourth chapter when I said stay away from futures and options strategies at first? I still mean it. But when you are ready to branch out into that area, you might want to learn from Minesh. Minesh is a cool cat. Ok, he's not really a cat. He's an expert options investor and he teaches one of the most easily executed and lower risk options strategies to consistently generate income from your gold or silver position. This is something you normally aren't able to do because investing in precious metals is a buy and hold deal. It's an advanced strategy that I, and many hedge funds, regularly use. Not for everyone. But if you have at least few thousand extra dollars to invest into ETFs and options, you should consider it. I touched on this strategy in Chapter Four where I said it was one of my only exceptions for using silver and gold ETFs. You can sign up for one of his free introductory webinars at: www.stacksilvergetgold.com/cashflowgold

STACK SILVER GET GOLD ONLINE TRAINING PROGRAM: I've received a ton of messages asking me to create an online video training program on the topics covered in this book. It seems some of you want a step by step training video version of this book. So that's what I made. Sometime in 2017, maybe by the time you read this, I will be launching an online video training course that will cover all the topics you've learned about so far and more. I'll also have live interviews with the people and businesses I've mentioned in this book as well as monthly question and answer sessions. Let me stress this point. The book you're reading right now is all you need to start safely buying gold and silver today. You do not need this course. But if you want to go a little deeper, you can sign up here: www.stacksilvergetgold.com/readerdiscount

GET A FREE STACK SILVER GET GOLD AUDIOBOOK: You've heard of Audible.com, right? They're the #1 audiobook seller in the world and I've partnered with them to get you the Stack Silver Get Gold audiobook for free. Here's the deal. As a bonus for signing up for a complimentary 30 day Audible membership trial, you'll get the Audible version of Stack Silver Get Gold for free. After your 30 day trial ends, they charge you $14.95 and you get one new audiobook of your choice each month. If you cancel your membership trial before 30 days is up, you never pay a dime and still get to keep Stack Silver Get Gold at no cost. I kept my membership though because audio books are efficient. With the audiobook version, you'll be able to listen to it in your car, on a plane or while working out or running. You'll really drill everything you need to know about precious metals permanently into your brain. To get your free Stack Silver Get Gold audiobook now, go here: www.stacksilvergetgold.com/audible

FINAL THOUGHT

Congrats on making it to the end! There are very few people in the world who realize the importance of owning gold and silver and you're smart enough to be one of them so welcome to the club! I believe the knowledge you have acquired from this book can make you money and protect you and your family from a devaluation of currency and a possible financial crisis and can also help protect and make others you know prosperous as well.

This book contains over a decade of expert precious metals investing knowledge and experience all boiled down to just over a hundred or so pages. It's really all you need. As for the people who say the dollar will never crash and blah blah blah, maybe that's true for the near term but remember chance favors the prepared mind. If you start stacking gold and silver and the world does change drastically, you'll be in good shape. If things go ok and the dollar does survive for another 25 years, guess what? Gold and silver are also commodities and their cyclical nature means if they're down now, they will be back up again in the future even without the doom and gloom happening. Either way, you'll be prepared.

So what I would do now if I were you is make a plan. Map out on paper the steps you're going to take to start stacking your gold and silver and building up your precious metals war chest. Are you going to go to a local dealer and make a big purchase first or use a private custodial dealer like OWNx and set up a monthly automated investing schedule to stack your metal? If I was starting all over from the beginning, here is what my plan would probably look like:

1) Set up an automated investing plan with OWNx to start disciplined investing in gold and silver once a month, even if it's only for $25 a pop. Just start. If you've got a good amount of money to invest, make a substantial purchase. Take delivery of some of it and let them store the rest for you in their private vault. I would make buying gold and silver a disciplined habit using dollar cost averaging.

2) Get familiar with local coin shops and dealers. Make a small purchase from each of them and see which one you like best. If you find a trustworthy dealer and he gives you a good price and doesn't murder you on mark up, make a larger purchase.

3) Set up some kind of home safe or good hiding place. It's perfectly ok if it's a small safe at first, like a book safe. You don't need Fort Knox.

4) Never stop learning. Get the books I have suggested at the library or on Amazon. Check out the bright minds and subscribe to their newsletters, email lists or listen to their podcasts. Follow me on Facebook at

www.facebook.com/silverinvesting or sign up for my online course.

5)   Once you've got a strategic war chest of gold and silver built up at home and in a private vault storage company in the United States, go offshore and set up a private safe deposit box.

6)   Never stop stacking gold and silver! Hold on to your physical gold and silver; don't sell it unless you absolutely have to for an emergency or if the price has gone to the moon. Real gold and silver is relatively rare compared to the amount traded in the paper markets. You want to hoard as much as you can! If you are certain the price will go down in the near future, instead of selling your physical metals, consider buying an inverse ETF as a hedge like I talked about in chapter eleven.

Please take one minute and help me spread the Stack Silver Get Gold word!

Few people know about investing in silver and gold and luckily you're one of them. If you thought this book did its job, please tell your friends about it, buy them a copy for a present or share it on your Facebook or Twitter pages. If you really enjoyed the book, one of the best things you can do to help me is take one minute now to review and rate it on Amazon.com.

I'm truly grateful for each and every one of you and I know if you implement what you just learned in the preceding pages, you'll know more than enough to successfully buy gold and silver bullion without getting ripped off. Please help spread this message and get others into buying gold and silver.

REVIEW. LIKE. RECOMMEND. SHARE. TELL.

Not sure how to post a review on Amazon.com? You can watch a short video showing you how to leave a review right here:

www.stacksilvergetgold.com/amazonreview

If you'd like to post a review or send others to my book, you'll find the direct links to my Amazon.com book listings here:

USA LISTING: www.stacksilvergetgold.com/amazon

UK LISTING: www.stacksilvergetgold.com/amazonuk

Thank you very much for reading my book! Now go implement what you've learned and buy some gold and silver bullion today!

The End.

DISCLAIMER

Investing involves risks and may not be suitable for everyone; you are urged to consult with your own financial advisors before making any investment decision. Past performance is not necessarily indicative of future results. Investing in precious metals often involves a degree of risk that makes them unsuitable for certain individuals. You should carefully consider the suitability of precious metals as a personal investment choice before taking any decisions that may affect your financial situation. This book makes no guarantees with respect to future price(s), or performance, of precious metals. Precious metals are not FDIC insured and may lose value. Companies, products, services and websites referred to by, or in any communications from, this book, are for educational, informational, and entertainment purposes only. The information in this book pertains to monetary history, the global economy, and the precious metals sector, and is not registered investment advice. Any information appearing in this book is not an endorsement or recommendation of any company or product and no representation is made, or advice given, regarding the advisability of purchasing products from, investing in, any company, product, service and website or purchasing or selling any security of any company. Readers should always conduct their own research and due diligence and obtain professional advice before making any investment decision. Disclosure of material connection: In this book, I suggest products and/or services for sale that are not my own and some of the links are affiliate links. My suggestion is ALWAYS based on my personal belief and or experience that the product, service or author will provide excellent and valuable information or services. This is based on my personal and professional relationship with that person or company, and/or a previous positive experience with the person or company whose product/service I am suggesting. In some cases, I will be compensated via a commission if you decide to purchase a product or service based on my suggestion. IMPORTANT: ALWAYS do your OWN due-diligence before making any purchases, whether I suggest them or not. THIS DISCLOSURE IS IN ACCORDANCE WITH THE FEDERAL TRADE COMMISSION'S 16 CFR, PART 255: "GUIDES CONCERNING THE USE OF ENDORSEMENTS AND TESTIMONIALS IN ADVERTISING."